Old Glasgow and Th

From the archives

Sandra Malcolm

Text © Sandra Malcolm 2005
Images © T. & R. Annan & Sons Ltd. 2005
First published in the United Kingdom, 2005,
by Stenlake Publishing Ltd.
Telephone: 01290 551122
www.stenlake.co.uk
Printed by Cordfall Ltd., Glasgow, G21 2QA

ISBN 1 84033 359 6

**Copies of the photographs featured in this book
may be obtained by contacting Douglas Annan:**

**The Annan Gallery
164 Woodlands Road
Glasgow G3 6LL
Telephone: 0141 332 0028
www.annangallery.co.uk**

West George Street, seen here in 1961, was originally called Camperdown Place, and along with St Vincent Place commemorated two of the Royal Navy's greatest victories. Most of the street was originally lined with terraced houses, built in the early 1800s. It contains many buildings of architectural interest, such as Connal's Building at No. 34, the dome of which features sculptures of locomotives and ships, along with carvings of James Watt, J. B. Neilson, William Dixon and Mr Connal himself. No. 62 is the Royal Faculty of Procurators building, dating from 1854 and designed by Charles Wilson. The Sun Fire & Life Building at 101 West George Street won its architect, William Leiper, a silver medal at the Paris Exhibition in 1900. In the distance is St George's Tron Parish Church.

Contents

Introduction

The firm of T. &. R. Annan & Sons Ltd., which celebrated its 150th anniversary in 2005, has long been a household name in Glasgow. It was established in 1855 by Thomas Annan (1829–1887), the son of a flax spinner and miller from Dairsie in Fife, who against his father's wishes apprenticed himself to a lithographer in Cupar and became a freehand copperplate engraver. The copperplate process was a means of producing prints (engravings) by etching a design onto a metal plate, which then had ink applied to it and was passed through rollers in contact with a sheet of paper. Once the plate had been etched (a time-consuming and skilled process), numerous prints could be produced quickly and cheaply.

In 1855 photography was in its infancy, but pioneers such as Thomas Annan rapidly realised the value of the medium's ability to capture real-world scenes and reproduce them repeatedly. Initially based at Woodlands Cottage in Woodlands Road,

Thomas Annan's original premises, Woodlands Cottage.

Thomas Annan.

T. & R. ANNAN & SONS.

PHOTOGRAPHERS &
PHOTOENGRAVERS
TO HER MAJESTY
THE QUEEN BY
SPECIAL APPOINT-
MENT
ELECTRIC LIGHT

REPRODUCTIONS OF
PAINTINGS IN
AUTOTYPE AND
PHOTOGRAVURE
BOOK ILLUSTRATIONS
ETC ETC
TELEPHONE NO 87

230 SAUCHIEHALL ST GLASGOW

T. & R. Annan & Sons was based at 230 Sauchiehall Street from 1882 to 1904.

Glasgow, Annan first described himself as a 'calotype printer'. Successful early photographers had to make their own negatives and other materials, and this required a good understanding of chemistry. The calotype process used paper negatives coated with silver iodide, and for a brief period Annan worked with a doctor called Berwick (first name unknown) who had an interest in chemistry.

Thomas Annan was clearly both talented and ambitious, quickly securing exclusive rights to a variety of new photographic processes. After only two years in business he relocated to more central premises at 116 Sauchiehall Street, with moves to 202 Hope Street and 153 Sauchiehall Street following in 1859 and 1873 respectively.

At its outset the business was largely based around photographing works of art and producing high-quality prints of these, something for which there was a ready market. Photography provided the means of capturing the original image, and Thomas Annan combined this with other processes that allowed superior quality prints to be made. In 1866 he secured the Scottish patent rights to Sir Joseph Wilson Swan's carbon printing process, leading to greater print permanence and the capture of more detail. On 27 March 1877 he was granted a deed of licence to practice the autotype and chromotype processes. The most important rights he secured, however, were those to heliogravure (later known as photogravure),

travelling to Vienna in 1883 with his nineteen-year-old son, James Craig, to be taught this process by its inventor, Karel Klic. Thomas Annan was granted the sole rights to heliogravure in Great Britain and Ireland, plus the right to sell the process to not more than two people.

Because the paintings he photographed were valuable and often bulky, Annan photographed them in situ at the houses of their wealthy owners, travelling across Scotland and Northern England in a blacked-out cab that doubled as a darkroom. He also photographed works of art held in public collections. These visits provided opportunities for additional commissions recording the exteriors and interiors of his clients' houses. As a result Annan came into contact with many of the most influential figures in Victorian Scotland, which undoubtedly helped to raise his profile and status. His experience of photographing country houses, and his pre-eminent position as a Glasgow-based photographer, made him the natural candidate to illustrate a prestigious volume entitled *The Old Country Houses of the Old Glasgow Gentry*, first published in 1870 (a revised edition followed in 1878). Annan may have even been able to recycle work that had already been commissioned privately during his country house visits. He was certainly well connected, both amongst the influential and the famous. In 1859 he and his family moved to Burnbank Road in Hamilton, where the firm's photographic printing works were also established.

David Livingstone's sisters lived next door, and Annan got to know the explorer during his visits, producing the definitive photographic portrait of him.

The house in Hamilton was called Talbot Cottage after William Henry Fox Talbot, the inventor of photography, and Thomas Annan knew David Octavius Hill (1802–1870), another highly influential figure in pioneer photography. In 1869 the Annans relocated to Rock House, Calton Hill, Edinburgh, the former premises and studio of David Octavius Hill. It is believed that this move was encouraged by the latter with a view to the Annans setting up an Edinburgh branch of their business, although the family had returned to Glasgow and then Hamilton within a year. In view of the large number of commissions Thomas Annan was already undertaking, it is doubtful whether he would have had time to manage a second studio.

In 1868, two years before his work on *The Old Country Houses of the Old Glasgow Gentry*, Thomas Annan produced the series of photographs for which he is best known. These were commissioned by Glasgow's City Improvement Trust and show buildings in and around High Street that had been compulsorily purchased and were due to be demolished. Many of the properties were slums, and the images provide a unique record of both historic buildings in the latter stages of dilapidation, and the living conditions of those for whom they were still places of work and abode. These did not appear in book form until 1900 when James Maclehose, publisher to the University of Glasgow, produced *The Old Closes & Streets of Glasgow*, including a number of later views which may have been taken by Thomas Annan's eldest son, John. The illustrations in the book are photogravure prints made by James Craig Annan (his second son) from Thomas Annan's negatives.

John Annan joined his father Thomas as a photographer in the business, and was followed by James Craig Annan in the late 1870s when he was still in his early teens. Thomas's brother Robert became a partner c.1873 in a solely administrative capacity. In 1877 the family home and company printing works were relocated to Lenzie, and after securing rights to the photogravure process in 1883 a significant amount of this work was carried out from there.

The premises at 202 Hope Street included a portrait studio, and while Thomas Annan specialised in taking portraits of eminent figures for publication, the general public could sit for cartes de visite. These small portraits, mounted on card,

T. & R. Annan were commercial photographers for whom portraits such as this one were an important source of business. Although the family looks respectable, scandal is hidden behind the pose. John Steven, the man with the beard, was born illegitimately in 1835 and brought up by his grandparents, possibly believing that his mother was his sister. His grandparents' names appear on his birth certificate, but his mother's name is on his death certificate. Despite difficult beginnings, John Steven became a signal superintendent for the Caledonian Railway in Glasgow. He and his wife Lilly had ten children, nine of whom survived to adulthood. A number of them moved abroad, but Alexander Steven followed in his father's footsteps, also becoming signal superintendent for the Caledonian Railway. John's great-grandson had a long career with the railway too.

were an affordable alternative for the photograph albums of the middle classes in an era when it was not practical for most people to take their own photographs.

Within twenty years of the firm's establishment, the exhibiting of fine art had been added to the range of photographic services offered. At the premises at 153 Sauchiehall Street a single prestigious painting would be hung in a dimly-lit, heavily curtained room to which members of the public were charged admission. James Craig Annan subsequently went on to introduce fine-art dealing to the business, selling original paintings alongside the firm's trademark prints.

Thomas Annan was undoubtedly a master photographer, who without first-class technical and artistic skills could not have achieved the success

that he did. He was also an extremely astute and energetic businessman. Victorian commercial photographers were numerous, and the fact that the name of Annan remains so well-known 150 years after the establishment of the company testifies to the quality of work and professionalism of its founder. His death in 1888 marked the end of an era, although the company that he had established continued to grow on the foundations he had laid.

Following Thomas Annan's death, James Craig Annan (1864–1946), then still in his early twenties, appears to have become the creative driving force behind the business. He was self-taught, learning the skills of photography and photogravure from his father and gleaning experience of the art world through contact with company clients, many of

Neilson & Co.'s Hydepark engineering works was founded in 1836 in Hydepark Street, Finnieston. Between 1844 and 1862, 429 locomotives were built at the works with the demand for engines so great that the owner, Walter Montgomerie Neilson, opened a new factory at Springburn in 1862, sandwiched between Cowlairs works, owned by the Edinburgh & Glasgow Railway, and the Caledonian

Railway's St Rollox works. Locomotives for export formed a major part of the business, with the first overseas order going to the Julian de Zulusta Railway in Havana in 1852. Completed engines were transported to the wharfs at Finnieston on low-loaders, where the giant Finnieston crane was used to lift them on to a suitable vessel. This picture dates from 1862.

whom were eminent artists and dealers. His personal friends included well-known contemporary artists, and in 1892 he exhibited his own landscape photographs of north Holland alongside etchings of the same country by D. Y. Cameron. In 1924 he became an Honorary Fellow of the Royal Photographic Society, and was made a Fellow of the Royal Society of Arts in 1936. James's brother John was also an important figure in the business, and was the senior partner after their father's death. He specialised in commercial photography, but also had an interest in painting and the art world.

Two important events in the company's history indicate its continuing success after Thomas Annan's death. In 1889 it was granted a Royal Warrant, and in 1904 it moved into prestigious

purpose-built premises at 518 Sauchiehall Street (having been based at 230 Sauchiehall Street since 1892). The new premises were designed by the firm of Honeyman, Keppie & Mackintosh, in which Charles Rennie Mackintosh was a partner, and indicate the interrelationships between many of Glasgow's leading businesses.

By 1920 the firm employed approximately 30 people, with a wide variety of work being undertaken. Thomas Craig Annan, John Annan's son, was the third generation family member to join the business, and as photogravure went into decline he developed the sale of colour prints from the early 1930s onwards. By 1937 this had become an important aspect of the business. He apparently had little interest in photography and his uncle James maintained the photographic studio until his

In the late nineteenth century Glasgow's civic leaders were looking for a site on which to create a new park for the east end of the city. Tollcross Estate was bought from James Dunlop, proprietor of the Clyde Ironworks, in 1897, and was opened as Tollcross Park by Lord Provost Sir David Richmond the same year. The purchase included Tollcross House and this gatehouse, along with other ancillary

buildings. Bailie A. G. Macdonald, an ex-convenor of the Parks Committee, presented his glasshouses and collection of plants, and for many years Tollcross House was used as a children's museum which included the legendary Cock Robin exhibit. This showed the unlucky robin and his cock sparrow murderer represented by stuffed birds. The exhibit remained on show until the museum closed in 1976.

Much of modern-day Queen's Park occupies the site of Camphill Farm. This was once owned by the Maxwell family, who sold it to Robert Thomson, a cotton manufacturer, in 1798. Through him it passed to James Oswald of Scotstoun in 1820. Camphill House was built on the site of the farmhouse, probably between 1820 and 1830, and Queen's Park's two ponds were excavated from its lawn in 1905. The path around the larger pond formed the main driveway to the mansion, which was turned into a museum in 1896, closing in the early 1980s. Camphill Gardens, seen here before 1905, are part of Queen's Park.

retirement in 1946. Thomas arranged exhibitions of the work of notable artists, including the Scottish Colourists.

The intervention of the Second World War signalled a gradual decline in the company's fortunes. John Craig Annan (Thomas's son) joined the company in 1937 but was called up in 1939. This prevented him from formally studying photography, and on his return from the war (by which time techniques and processes would have moved on considerably) he took overall responsibility for the business, with fine art dealing growing in importance and photography waning. From 1946, the year of James Craig Annan's death,

no member of the family was a photographer, although photographic staff were still employed. The firm became a limited company the same year and has traded as T. & R. Annan & Sons Ltd. ever since.

In 1959, after 55 years at 518 Sauchiehall Street, the company relocated to smaller premises at 130 West Campbell Street, and at this stage the majority of old glass plates, plus numerous prints of historical interest that could no longer be stored, were lost. By the 1970s art dealing was the key area of business, and in 1973 it was recorded that photography 'is now the least rewarding of the company's activities and of minor concern.

Renfrew airport began life as an aerodrome for the Royal Flying Corps during the First World War. Between 1925 and 1933 No. 602 (City of Glasgow) Auxiliary Air Force Squadron trained there, and during the Second World War air services at Renfrew linked countries as part of the National Air Communications System under the control of the Air Ministry. Because of its proximity to the docks in Glasgow, hundreds of aircraft were assembled or repaired there. In 1947 Renfrew became the headquarters of the Scottish division of British European Airways, although even by then the site had become too small. It was enlarged by absorbing the major part of an adjoining golf course, and on 26 November 1954 Renfrew's new terminal building (seen here in 1955) was opened. This was designed by Sir William Hardie Kininmonth and survived until 1978 when it was demolished to make way for a supermarket development. Even as early as the 1950s plans were being mooted for a new airport which would allow bigger aircraft to land. The site at Abbotsinch had been used as an RAF training station from 1932 to 1943, after which it was transferred to Royal Naval Air Service use. It was developed as the new airport, opening on 27 June 1966.

Nevertheless the studio is still used occasionally for portraiture and the firm continue to take photographs, as needed, for the National Gallery of Scotland.'

Whilst the taking of photographs eventually ceased completely as a commercial activity in the late 1970s, T. & R. Annan & Sons is still a well-respected name in Glasgow today, trading as fine art dealers and framers from premises in the West End on Woodlands Road, close to where the company was founded in 1855. Several hundred prints illustrating some of T. & R. Annan's most famous work are on display and available for sale. Since the 1980s the business has been run by Douglas Annan, who took over the reins from his father and is a fifth-generation family member.

The contribution that T. & R. Annan has made to photographic history both in Scotland and further afield should not be underestimated. Not only did the company produce two internationally renowned photographers, but the surviving body of work – included in numerous public and private collections – provides a vivid insight into the life and culture of Glasgow and the West of Scotland from the mid-nineteenth century until after the end of the Second World War. The diversity of T. & R. Annan's output is illustrated in the range of photographs featured in this book.

131 Gallowgate, 1868.

Chapter 1
High Street and medieval Glasgow

T. & R. Annan's best-known series of photographs are those showing High Street, Trongate, Saltmarket and Gallowgate in the late nineteenth century. They reveal the city centre during a period of dramatic change, often featuring medieval buildings that had by then disintegrated into slums.

Prior to the Industrial Revolution, High Street and the surrounding area was characterised by orchards, gardens and green spaces. Rapid development and population growth changed the character of the area dramatically, leading the writer Hugh MacDonald to describe High Street as 'squalid and repulsive' in 1853. By this time the expansion of the West End was beginning to fuel an exodus of the middle classes from the city centre, with immigrant workers filling the vacuum. Between 1775 and 1861 Glasgow underwent a six-fold population explosion.

In 1839 the author of a Parliamentary Report on Housing in Great Britain stated: 'I have seen human degradation in some of the worst places, both in England and abroad, but I did not believe until I had visited the wynds of Glasgow that so large an amount of filth, crime, misery and disease existed in one spot in any civilised country'. In 1842 a report on the Sanitary Conditions of the Labouring Population was similarly damning. It recorded that: 'In the courts of Argyle Street there were no privies or drains and the dung heaps received all the filth which the swarms of wretched inhabitants could

give'. In the four months between December 1848 and March 1849, 43,000 Irish immigrants settled in the city, while in 1853–4 a cholera epidemic (Glasgow's third) killed 100 people per 1,000 of the city's population. High Street and its environs formed the epicentre of this picture of overcrowding, squalor and disease.

Soon after 1846 the town council started to buy up dilapidated property around High Street in an effort to reduce the amount of poor housing stock, but builders quickly erected new and equally crowded properties on neighbouring sites. The council used the opportunities afforded by the expansion of the railways in the city centre to apply for powers under the City Improvement Act, a piece of slum clearance legislation with jurisdiction across the whole of the United Kingdom. This led to the City of Glasgow Improvement Act of 1866, which authorised Glasgow Town Council to clear more than 90 acres of land in Trongate, Saltmarket, Gallowgate and High Street. In 1868 Thomas Annan was commissioned by the associated City Improvement Trust to take a series of photographs of the closes and wynds earmarked for demolition.

The Act stated that 39 new streets were to be laid out, twelve existing ones altered, and the cleared ground sold or leased to private owners for the building of property to standards approved by the Trustees of the Act. By 1874 the City Improvement Trust had 'demolished the houses of some 15,425 persons', but three years later the demand for land had dwindled and the Trust could no longer sell the sites it cleared. Since it had no other source of income, it was unable to improve the remaining areas under its schedule and in effect became a slum landlord itself.

In 1889 the Trust started building new housing, and by 1902 the work of the 1866 Act was finished. By this time the City Improvement Trust had built 1,646 houses plus 394 shops and other commercial premises. Ultimately, however, the new buildings did not solve Glasgow's slum problem, which was simply transferred to different areas, and in the end the buildings erected by the Trust became slums themselves, although largely through obsolescence rather than decay.

The bulk of the images in this chapter date from 1868 and were produced by Thomas Annan for the City Improvement Trust. Some later photographs may have been taken by Thomas's son John prior to the publication of *The Old Closes & Streets of Glasgow* in 1900. Collectively, they provide a vivid picture of the medieval city in the closing decades of the nineteenth century.

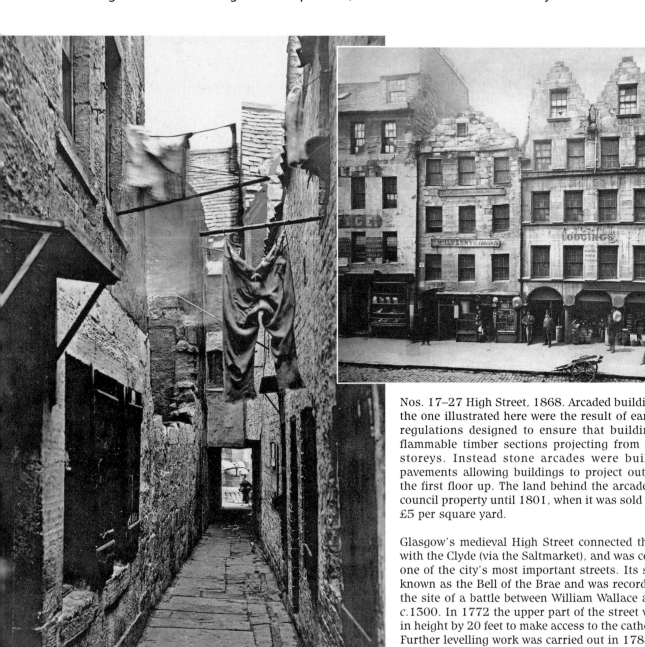

Nos. 17–27 High Street, 1868. Arcaded buildings such as the one illustrated here were the result of earlier council regulations designed to ensure that buildings had no flammable timber sections projecting from their upper storeys. Instead stone arcades were built over the pavements allowing buildings to project outwards from the first floor up. The land behind the arcades remained council property until 1801, when it was sold for shops at £5 per square yard.

Glasgow's medieval High Street connected the cathedral with the Clyde (via the Saltmarket), and was consequently one of the city's most important streets. Its summit was known as the Bell of the Brae and was recorded as being the site of a battle between William Wallace and his foes c.1300. In 1772 the upper part of the street was reduced in height by 20 feet to make access to the cathedral easier. Further levelling work was carried out in 1783 and again a few years later, although plans to complete this work and straighten the line of the street in 1800 never went ahead. This wynd at 101 High Street was photographed in 1868.

Bell Street from High Street, 1868.

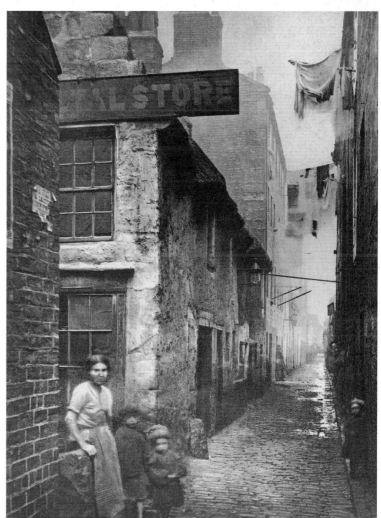

A vennel off High Street, 1868.

Vennel, 65 High Street, 1868.

High Street, 1868, looking south
towards the Tolbooth.

16

Broad Close, 167 High Street, 1868.

Photographed in 1897, these tenements at the corner of Duke Street and High Street were cleared as part of the City Improvement Trust's work, as were those at the corner of George Street and High Street. Duke Street is the longest street in Britain, and is said to be named after the Duke of Montrose, who had lodgings that overlooked it. It is probably most famous (or infamous) for the prison that was once situated on it, which was both the main jail for Glasgow and the women's prison for the West of Scotland. It bore a flagpole on which a black flag was hoisted when someone was hanged there. Other landmarks on Duke Street included the Great Eastern Hotel, the cattle market, a horse bazaar, meat market and greyhound track.

The 1897 photograph below shows the line of High Street (left) leading diagonally towards the centre of the picture, then continuing southwards to the Tolbooth. George Street branches off to the right. At the right-hand edge of the picture is the steeple of the Ramshorn Kirk in Ingram Street. During the early nineteenth century, the church's graveyard was regularly raided by bodysnatchers engaged in the profitable trade of supplying corpses to anatomists. Bodies were snatched from the Ramshorn despite numerous precautions, which included the posting of guards, relatives standing watch at night, alarm wires being installed around new graves and heavy stones being placed over them. The Anatomy Act of 1832 extended the legal availability of cadavers for medical research and education, and essentially put an end to grave-robbing.

Back Wynd, photographed in 1899, was typical of the narrow thoroughfares that developed behind tenements and other buildings facing the city's principal streets in this crowded part of the city.

Bishop Andrew Muirhead built Provand's Lordship in the fifteenth century as part of the St Nicholas Hospital, an almshouse for the poor. It provided accommodation for twelve men who lived and worked in the hospital, studied the Bible and tended its herb garden. Provand's Lordship was one of a number of buildings associated with the clergy and was at one time occupied by the Lord Prebend of Barlanark. This title later became 'Lord of Provan' leading to 'Provand's Lordship'. In the early twentieth century the ancient building was occupied by Isaac Morton, who ran a sweet shop and mineral water business on the ground floor and lived with his family in the rest of the premises. To combat the threat of demolition, the Provand's Lordship Society was formed in 1906, with Sir William Burrell a leading campaigner to save the house. He provided furniture and furnishings illustrating how it would have looked in the seventeenth century. After the Mortons moved out of the building in 1918 it became a museum. This photograph was taken in 1900.

The origins of the University of Glasgow can be traced to a papal bull of 7 January 1451, obtained by William Turnbull, Bishop of Glasgow, from Pope Nicholas V. The bull stated, amongst other things, that Glasgow was admirably fitted to be the home of a university because of its temperate climate and 'abundance of victuals'. Until the first university building was erected in High Street in 1453, business was conducted in the cathedral crypt or chapter-house. In 1460 Lord Hamilton donated a small tenement on the east side of High Street, north of Blackfriars, and seven years later an adjoining property was given by Thomas of Arthurlie. The faculty built its 'Pedagogy' or College of the Faculty of Arts here, and it was on the same site, extended by a gift from Queen Mary, that the buildings illustrated were constructed during the seventeenth century. Described at the time as 'the chief ornament of the city', they were known as the Old College and remained in use until the university moved to Gilmorehill in 1870. The main structure, two conjoined quadrangles, was completed soon after 1632. Although the tower was finished in 1658 it was not until the 1690s that the clock was added, along with a balustrade for the staircase leading from the outer quadrangle to the Fore Hall. By 1694 the university had 250 students, rising to 400 in 1702. Only 40 students lived in by 1704, at which point Glasgow ceased to be a residential university.

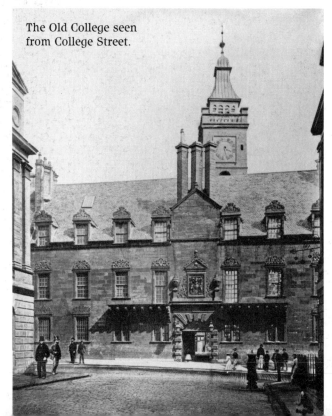

The Old College seen from College Street.

Old College, Inner Court.

The Lion and Unicorn staircase was moved from the Old College to Gilmorehill in 1872. It is seen here in its original location.

The Royal Infirmary was founded beside Glasgow Cathedral in 1792. Earlier hospitals in the city, such as the St Nicholas Hospital and Hutcheson's Hospital, didn't generally offer medical treatment and were really places of rest for the aged poor. The impetus for the building of the infirmary came not from a doctor, but from the then Professor of Logic at Glasgow University, George Jardine. He was secretary of the infirmary until 1815. Another non-medical man, Professor Meileman, Chair of Natural Philosophy, succeeded him. Wealthy city merchants supported the infirmary, with its first major benefactor being David Dale. This building was designed by Robert and James Adam, but very quickly became too small for the needs of a rapidly expanding city, with numerous extensions built. Joseph Lister first began the antiseptic treatment of wounds with carbolic acid at the infirmary. Unfortunately his male accident ward was built over a burial ground containing coffins of the victims of the cholera epidemic of 1849, separated from the ward above by a mere four feet of earth. In addition it was discovered that at least 5,000 paupers' bodies had been piled into mass graves in the neighbouring old cathedral churchyard, adding to the health risks. The Dean of Guild ordered that these be treated with carbolic acid and quicklime to reduce mortality rates in the infirmary. In 1907 the Adam building (illustrated here) was replaced by a new structure designed by James Miller.

Waiting room, Royal Infirmary.

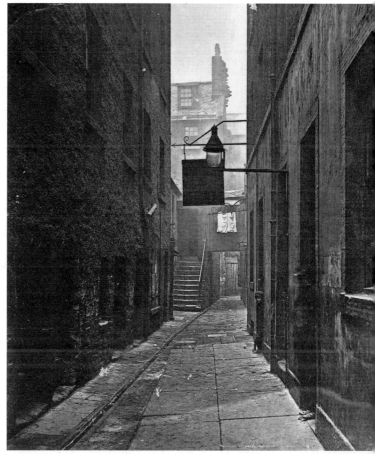

Above: Closes at 97 and 103 Saltmarket. Glasgow's Saltmarket has enjoyed mixed fortunes over the centuries. In *Rob Roy*, Sir Walter Scott refers to 'A' the comforts o' the Sautmarket', and when Daniel Defoe walked down the street he was able to enjoy uninterrupted views of the Clyde and its green banks. By the time Thomas Annan photographed its closes and vennels in 1868 it was anything but comfortable, and had a reputation as 'a citadel of vice'. In an area of less than a sixteenth of a square mile there were 150 shebeens and 200 brothels.

Above right: No. 18 Saltmarket, 1868. Salt sold at the market after which the street was named was primarily used for the curing of salmon fished from the Clyde. As Glasgow grew, the salmon curers moved to where the Molendinar Burn joined the Clyde, and buildings were then erected on the west side of the Saltmarket. At one time the street was favoured by the wealthy: Oliver Cromwell had his lodgings there and Provost Bell had a house in Saltmarket in which King James VII stayed. When Cromwell visited Glasgow he worshipped at the cathedral, and during a service there the preacher denounced him as an enemy to the true faith. One of Cromwell's officers asked for permission to shoot him, but Cromwell had his own method of revenge. He invited the preacher to dinner, and after it was over engaged him in prayer for no less than three hours.

Right: 136 Saltmarket, 1868. Until 1750 all Scotland's banks had their headquarters in Edinburgh, but the following year Glasgow's first bank was founded in the Saltmarket. Called the Glasgow & Ship Bank, it was located at the corner of Saltmarket and Bridgegate, later moving to the Trongate. The city's first post office was opened in the Saltmarket *c.*1710.

No. 28 Saltmarket. The buildings shown in these 1868 photographs were subsequently demolished under the Glasgow City Improvement Act of 1866.

Saltmarket from London Road, 1885. According to Bailie Nicol Jarvie (a character from Sir Walter Scott's *Rob Roy*) 'the douce Glasgow merchants of the olden times won their crowns, kept their crowns, and counted their crowns' in the Saltmarket. The city's first coffee house stood at the corner of Saltmarket and Trongate and was later used as a book auction room by the Foulis brothers, printers to the university. St Andrew's Parish Church, the kirk of Glasgow Town Council, stood just out of view to the left. In 1805, when Dr William Ritchie was appointed minister, he found a small organ in the church that had been made by James Watt. He allowed this to be used at choir practice, although ordinary services had a precentor who led the choir and congregation without the aid of an organ. The following year the church elders and Dr Ritchie petitioned Glasgow Town Council to be allowed to move some seats in the church so that the organ could be used for services. The council refused, but in 1807 the church members decided to defy its ruling and an organist played music for the final psalm. This act led the presbytery to announce that organ music was 'contrary to the law of the land' and the offending item was removed, ultimately coming to rest in the People's Palace.

Saltmarket photographed from the Bridgegate. Also known as the Briggait, this street branches off the western side of the Saltmarket and was the route to the first bridge over the Clyde in Glasgow. Sir William Bruce constructed the Merchants' House on the Briggait, and great assemblies and balls were held there. Its allure lasted 100 years before the merchants began to move out, and after being sold in 1871 it was demolished. Thirty years earlier Irish immigrants began to arrive in Glasgow as they escaped the potato famine. It was said that those who could afford it went to America, those with only a little money travelled to Liverpool, and those with no money at all came to Glasgow. The fare from Belfast to the Broomielaw was fourpence per person. Many of the Irish moved into deserted merchants' mansions in the Briggait leading to vast overcrowding in the area.

King Street (seen here in 1868) was the location of the city's first market and appears on maps from c.1720. It contained some fine buildings, but many became slums as the railways began to extend into the area. The street's Institution Tavern was popular with university students and professors, with Sir Walter Scott claiming that it was his favourite tavern in Glasgow and often tying his horse up at the door. The building had a low roof, the floors were sanded and all the drink was served in silver tankards. It also had a wishing stone – according to legend, if you sat below this stone and had a drink your wish would come true. This photograph appears to have been taken looking northwards into Candleriggs, with the tower of the Ramshorn Kirk just visible in the distance.

John Jackson's theatre in Dunlop Street opened in 1782, and until 1797 was 'a second home' to Edinburgh's Theatre Royal. In 1804 George IV granted a patent for a Theatre Royal in Glasgow, and Jackson and his partner Aitken established this the following year in Queen Street, just to the north of the Stirling Library. In 1818 it became the first theatre in Britain to be 'illuminated with sparkling gas'. However, its ornate decor and extensive size meant that it was never a commercial success, and it burnt down in 1829 due to leaking joints in the pipes carrying the 'sparkling gas'. After Jackson moved his enterprise to Queen Street, the Dunlop Street theatre was renamed

the Caledonian and staged musical entertainments, circus shows and equestrian dramas. In 1825 a battle began between J. H. Alexander, the lessee of the Caledonian, and a rival theatre operator called Frank Seymour. When Alexander lost the lease of the Caledonian to his rival he immediately rented the cellar under the theatre. Both men put on opposing shows on the same nights: for example, if one was staging a romantic drama, the other might hire a brass band. Glasgow audiences loved the altercations and turned up in their thousands, drawing more business away from the Theatre Royal in Queen Street. When this burned down J. H. Alexander bought the patent and transferred it to Dunlop Street, rebuilding the former Caledonian as the Theatre Royal. It remained at this location until 1869. In

1849 a false fire alarm led to the death of 70 people in a stampede. Alexander, who retired in 1851, is buried in the Necropolis in a tomb complete with proscenium arch. After his death the theatre was run by the Glover family until it burned down in 1863. It was rebuilt but subsequently demolished to make way for St Enoch Station. The title was then transferred to a theatre in Cowcaddens Street, but in 1879 it too burnt down. Three years later it opened again, only to burn down in 1895. Having reopened for a second time it managed to survive until the 1950s, when it was bought by Scottish Television. The present Theatre Royal is in Hope Street. This Annan photograph is captioned 'Theatre Royal, Dunlop Street' and is likely to show the building as it appeared after rebuilding in 1863.

Glasgow Green covers 136 acres and was granted to Bishop William Turnbull by James II in 1450 for use as common grazing ground. The 144-foot column in the middle of the picture commemorates the naval victories of Admiral Lord Nelson, and was erected by public subscription in 1806. The insult 'You'll die facing the monument' refers to the fact that public hangings took place on scaffolding built at the entrance to the South Jail, on Jail Square at the end of the Green. The last person to be hanged in

Glasgow was Dr Pritchard, who had poisoned his wife and mother-in-law in his house in Sauchiehall Street. 30,000 people came to view his execution on 28 July 1865. The Green has long been a focus for Glasgow Fair entertainments, with circuses, freak shows, pie shops, wrestlers' booths, oyster stalls, geggies, beer tents, performing bears, waxworks and whisky vendors formerly

amongst the delights to be sampled. The distinctive outline of Templeton's carpet factory can be seen in the left background. Designed by William Leiper, this was erected between 1889 and 1892 in the style of the Doge's Palace in Venice. During construction the facade collapsed in high winds and 29 women and girls working in the weaving sheds were killed.

Main Street, Gorbals, photographed from the corner of Rutherglen Road looking south in 1868, only a short time before the buildings were swept away by the City Improvement Trust. The earliest mention of a village on the lands of Gorbals dates to 1285, and the settlement was commonly known as Brigend or Bridge End until well into the eighteenth century. During the early fourteenth century a lepers' hospital was founded there, but this had become a general hospital by the time of its demolition in 1730.

To the north of the area seen in the upper photograph was a piece of land owned by George Elphinstone. He converted the chapel associated with the former lepers' hospital into a private chapel for his family, and built a mansion house adjacent to it known as the Elphinstone Tower, facing the village main street. Both tower and chapel were sold by the council to John Lawson in 1827, with the former subdivided into flats and stripped of its balustrades and turrets at the same time. The chapel became a pub called the Old Gorbals Wine and Spirit Vaults, as seen here in 1868.

This property is situated about one mile eastward from the Cross, on the north side of the old highway to Edinburgh, now Eastern Gallowgate. It was once a beautiful suburban villa, embosomed in trees, and perfectly retired. But the unceasing extension of the City has reached that district, and completely changed its rural character. The grounds are now intersected by streets; both sides of the old highway built; and all that is at present recognizable of the Annfield of olden time is the house itself, yet lingering in a new street leading up to it from Gallowgate, but doomed to early demolition. The aspect, in a forlorn state, has been preserved in the photograph.

Chapter 2
Glasgow's mansion houses

Aside from his work for the City Improvement Trust, Thomas Annan's other major commission of the 1860s was a series of photographs for an important historical volume, *The Old Country Houses of the Old Glasgow Gentry*. This was quite different in character from the Improvement Trust commission, focusing on the architectural heritage of Glasgow's magnates and merchants, as opposed to recording inner-city slum dwellings. There was a similarity, however, in that a number of the houses featured had been demolished by the time of publication, and others were under threat of imminent destruction.

The first edition appeared in 1870, a labour of love compiled by John Guthrie Smith, John Oswald Mitchell and John Buchanan. A selection of 100 houses was made, with Annan's photographic prints glued into each copy. Choosing only 100 buildings inevitably meant that the work was not comprehensive, with the criteria for inclusion sometimes unclear. Palatial dwellings and relatively minor houses appear alongside each other, and a number of seemingly important mansions are missed out.

Although the subject matter differed vastly from that of the City Improvement Trust photographs, the motivations of the authors and publishers were similar: to record elements of Glasgow that were rapidly changing. The book was presented as a social commentary as much as a historical one,

with much heart-searching about the rise of the new school of wealthy but socially detached businessmen, alongside an acknowledgement of the shortcomings of the previously dominant aristocrats. In their introduction the authors lamented that 'Now-a-days, our leading merchant has too often ceased to be a citizen', noting that the children of such men tended to be sent to England to be educated and as a result were 'rather ashamed of having anything to do with the big smoky town'.

When the second, revised edition was published in 1878 it was noted that 'Glasgow looks almost as new as Chicago', and had 'seen great changes since this book was published eight years ago'. Some different photographs were included (although the total number of houses was still limited to 100), sometimes for what seem to be political reasons – an unflattering view of someone's house might be replaced by a more appealing one.

Photography has long been celebrated as a documentary medium, and as Glasgow's leading commercial photographer Thomas Annan was a natural choice for illustrating *The Old Country Houses of the Old Glasgow Gentry*. Once again, his photographs formed a vital record of the changing city and its expanding boundaries. The following pages illustrate a few of the houses featured in the 1878 edition.

Bellahouston or Dumbreck House stood in Govan Parish on a small hill, commanding 'a beautiful and extensive view in all directions'. In 1595 a number of heritors in Govan who had previously been tenants of the Archbishopric of Glasgow obtained a charter of confirmation of their lands from James VI, with the intention that this would lead them to improve their properties. It is thought that the lands of Dumbreck were among those included. At the end of the eighteenth century these belonged to William Woddrop, who built the house illustrated here. On his death they passed to his nephew, Robert Scot of the Thistle Bank, who sold the house and

Opposite: The lands of Craigend originally formed part of the Barony of Mugdock, and almost every visitor to modern-day Mugdock Country Park will recognise the ruins of Craigend Castle. When the 2nd Marquis of Montrose had to sell off parts of Mugdock to pay family debts in the seventeenth century, a portion of land was bought by Robert Smith. Towards the end of the eighteenth century, John Smith, 'a West India proprietor and merchant in Glasgow', built a 'plain square house' on the site of Craigend Castle. The building illustrated here was built by his son, James Smith, and included part of its predecessor. James died in 1838 and was succeeded by his son, John, who in 1851

lands to a Mr Steven of Bellahouston. He changed the name from Dumbreck to that of his larger estate. Bellahouston had formerly belonged to an old Govan family called Rowan, of whom Thomas Rowan was the last of the line. It descended to the Steven family through marriage. The authors of *The Old Country Houses of the Old Glasgow Gentry* recorded that 'Within the last few years, great changes have taken place on the estate of Bellahouston, streets have been formed, and villas and country houses erected, in many parts of it, by merchants of the neighbouring city'. The house stood on land which now forms part of Bellahouston Park.

sold the estate to Sir Andrew Buchanan, whose family had also been merchants in Glasgow. James Outram, owner of the *Glasgow Herald*, leased Craigend in the early twentieth century, then Sir Harold Yarrow of the Yarrow's shipbuilding empire moved there in 1920. In 1949, having fallen upon harder times, the property became part of a zoo owned by William Wilson & Son, who also had a miniature zoo in Oswald Street. The star attraction was Charlie the elephant, but the zoo was not a commercial success and closed in September 1954. Charlie and his mahout Ibrahim moved to Filey in Yorkshire after spending some time at Butlins in Ayr.

The 'very handsome and commodious edifice' of Killermont House can still be seen today as the clubhouse and headquarters of the Glasgow Golf Club. In the seventeenth century the Killermont estate was owned by the Cunninghams of Drumquhassil, but in 1628 John Cunningham sold it to John Stark for 12,000 merks. The latter was a Covenanter and as such refused to conform to the Episcopal form of church government and worship. Despite being described as 'Younger of Killermont' in 1685, the estate had actually been sold to James Hunter of Muirhouse at least a year beforehand. It changed hands again in 1747 when Lawrence Colquhoun, the second son of Andrew Colquhoun of Garscadden, became the new owner. Lawrence's daughter Agnes married John Campbell of Clathic, and their son, Archibald Campbell Colquhoun, became Sheriff of Perthshire, Lord Advocate, Lord Clerk

Register and MP for Dumbartonshire (sic). He was also a partner in the Thistle Bank of Glasgow. The house and grounds became the home of Glasgow Golf Club in 1904.

Yorkhill House stood 'on the south side of the old road leading to Partick, a short distance beyond the point where it diverges from the new one ... on an eminence, overlooking an extensive and picturesque landscape'. The ancient name of this area was Over Newton, which extended to 60 acres and included some of Kelvinhaugh, reaching east as far as Stobcross. During the early eighteenth century Over Newton belonged to Crawford of Milton and then passed to George Bogle and Robert Barclay, two prominent Glasgow citizens, who put it up for sale in 1777. By the beginning of the nineteenth century it was in the possession of Robert Fulton Alexander, and in 1805 he built the mansion seen here. The house and grounds were sold to Andrew Gilbert, a Glasgow merchant, in 1813, who also purchased other land adjoining it, expanding what by then had become known as the Yorkhill Estate. His niece inherited the property from him and she and her husband added a new wing to the house.

The estate of Mount Vernon was in the parish of Old Monkland, near Baillieston. Its ancient name was 'Windy-edge', which it retained until c.1756, when a Glasgow merchant, George Buchanan, bought it from Adam Fairholm and built the oldest part of the mansion seen here, giving both house and estate the name Mount Vernon. In 1827 wings were added and the interior altered and 'modernised'. George Buchanan was the second son of Provost Andrew Buchanan of Drumpellier, who made his fortune from tobacco. Mount Vernon was George's country residence, and to complement this he had a spacious town house at the top of Virginia Street, said to be 'one of the most splendid private residences … in Glasgow'. Although he died a young man in 1762, aged only 34, George Buchanan had amassed a fortune from the Virginia trade by that time. His son, Andrew Buchanan, was not so astute, and had to sell the Virginia Street mansion to Alexander Spiers of Elderslie in 1770. When he died heirless in 1795 the line was continued by his brother David, who in addition to being a much more successful businessman benefited from a 'great windfall', when in 1821 he inherited the bulk of the wealth of Robert 'Robin' Carrick of the Ship Bank in Bridgegate. In later years Mount Vernon was occupied by Charles Gairdner, head of the Union Bank of Scotland, but the estate was gradually eaten away by the erection of villas, beginning in 1860. Mount Vernon Station on the Glasgow, Bothwell, Hamilton and Coatbridge line opened in 1883 making access to and from the city easier, and the estate was gradually feued with new streets and houses. The house was demolished in 1932.

Opposite: In 1691 the Scotstoun Estate was bought by William Walkinshaw, a Jacobite, who built Scotstoun House at the beginning of the eighteenth century. He had to flee the country after the 1715 rebellion, at which point the 9th Earl of Eglinton claimed the seat as his. In 1751 Richard and Alexander Oswald bought the estate. Their family had come from Caithness and they traded to Virginia, the West Indies and Madeira. Being very wealthy they built themselves 'Oswald's Land' in the Stockwell in 1742, 'for their house and their counting-house, with great cellars below for the Tobacco and the Madeira'. Described as 'kindly, hospitable, and generous old bachelors, with a special warm side to any one from Caithness', both men died at Scotstoun – in 1763 and 1766 – after which the estate passed to a more distant relation, George Oswald, a tobacco importer and partner in the Ship Bank. In 1822 it was inherited by Elizabeth Oswald, and the front of the house, looking towards the river, was added in 1825 on her instructions to designs by David Hamilton. She lived at Scotstoun for her entire 98 years and made generous financial contributions to the area. When she died in 1864 an inventory was taken before the estate passed to her great nephew, James Gordon, and this provides a detailed picture of what the interior of Scotstoun House would have looked like at the time. Neither James Gordon nor his son ever lived at Scotstoun, preferring to spend time on their estate at Aigas in Invernesshire. The house was demolished to make way for the railway line between Glasgow and Helensburgh/Balloch.

Renfield Street, 1936.

Chapter 3
The Victorian city centre

At the same time as the City Improvement Trust was carrying out its programme of slum clearance and redevelopment around High Street, Glasgow's Victorian commercial centre was emerging along new and thoroughly modern lines further to the west. Fuelled by a prodigious growth in manufacturing and commerce, Glasgow consolidated its position as a global centre of trade and industry as the nineteenth century progressed. Buildings on a scale not previously seen were erected on wide streets laid out in formal grid patterns, housing the offices of companies which manufactured and traded products of every description across the globe.

With the development of the railway network, long-distance travel became faster and cheaper, and hotels sprung up to cater for a new breed of businessman, the commercial traveller. Thomas Annan's images of George Square show it encircled with hotels to cater for this new market – as well as tourists and other visitors to the city.

The bulk of the images in this chapter illustrate those parts of Glasgow that lie to the west of High Street, extending as far as Charing Cross, and date from the 1870s to the 1960s. Photographs of

Glasgow Cross, Gallowgate and Trongate form a link between medieval Glasgow and its Victorian counterpart. In many instances the locations are immediately recognisable, but at the same time significantly different from their modern equivalents. Both Buchanan Street and Sauchiehall Street are seen prior to pedestrianisation, with St Enoch Square still dominated by the bulk of its train station and hotel. Trams form the principal mode of transport, and amongst the shops and businesses are modern-day survivors such as Fraser's, along with familiar names from the past such as Paisley's.

Buildings and streetscapes that to twenty-first century eyes now seem historic were strikingly modern when first constructed. The iron-framed Gardner's Warehouse on Jamaica Street, for instance, embodied a radically new style of architecture when it was built almost 150 years ago, but paved the way for further generations of contemporary architecture. The craftsmanship of Glasgow's Victorian builders and stonemasons – who incorporated elaborate symbolic carvings into the detail of their buildings – is captured in the equally skilled photography of Thomas Annan and his successors.

By the 1750s the number of taverns and inns in the city was increasing steadily as Glasgow's merchants created a demand for their services. The city's first hotel was the Saracen's Head in Gallowgate, which was opened in 1755 by the brewer Robert Tennant and featured a large function room in which 100 people could be entertained. In 1760 the Black Bull Inn in Argyle Street opened. The Tontine Hotel was the first hotel that really catered for travellers, also containing a coffee room for subscribers and an assembly hall. The eastern end of the building had been completed by 1737 and the west end by 1760. In 1781 the Tontine Society bought the premises, converting them into the hotel seen here. Glasgow's Tobacco Lords (as the magnates who dealt in this trade were known) used the hotel, and the coffee house was a recognised place of business. As the city's commercial centre moved west, Glasgow Cross declined as a business district and the Tontine was abandoned as a hotel in the 1850s. The building was turned into shops and offices, but was destroyed by fire in 1912.

Five streets meet at Glasgow Cross: High Street, Gallowgate, London Road, Saltmarket and Trongate. High Street was the city's medieval heart, connecting the Cross to the cathedral; Gallowgate formed the route to Edinburgh, passing Gallows Muir; London Road led (eventually) to England; the Saltmarket was where the salt sellers traded; and Trongate led to Dumbarton and the west. The Tolbooth steeple, designed by John Boyd and built between 1625 and 1627, originally formed part of a much larger building. This accommodated the town clerk's office, the council hall, jail and courthouses. Proclamations were made from a specially built platform outside and the area around the Tolbooth was also used for executions and pillories. The southern end of High Street was eventually widened when the Druids Halls, seen here, were demolished and replaced by the concave building seen on the facing page. This was completed in 1927 and allowed traffic to flow round either side of the Tolbooth steeple.

The original mercat cross was removed from Glasgow Cross in 1659 and the building seen here erected in 1929, a gift to the city from Dr William Black and his wife. It consists of an octagonal tower with a pillar rising from it. Atop the pillar is a heraldic unicorn holding a shield. The tower below features plaques bearing the arms of Scotland and Glasgow.

Gallowgate (seen here c.1905) leads east from Glasgow Cross and from the mid-eighteenth century was a centre of industrial activity, with dyeworks, potteries, tanneries and breweries situated along its length. In the 1950s there were 60 pubs in the street and in Victorian days it was notorious for its thieves and prostitutes. Until after the Second World War it was home to the Queen's Theatre, which produced pantomimes with a reputation for their 'earthy' humour. Just behind the theatre was a blacksmith's shop where the smith specialised in singeing sheep's heads for hotels and restaurants in Glasgow. It perished in a fire along with the theatre. Further east along the street was the Saracen's Head Inn, built using stone from the old Bishop's Castle. In 1773 Samuel Johnstone and James Boswell stayed at the hotel after their tour of the Hebrides. It was subsequently converted into a tenement and in 1904 was sold for demolition. When it was taken down in 1905 some skeletons were discovered, buried in what was the remains of the churchyard of Little St Mungo's Chapel.

The original name of Trongate was St Thenew's Gait, meaning the way to St Thenew's Chapel (Thenew was St Mungo's mother). In 1491 the Bishop of Glasgow negotiated the right to have a free tron, or weighing machine, located in Glasgow, at which goods coming into the city were weighed and customs collected. The tron was situated in Trongate, hence the street's change of name. Customs collected went to the bishop, and through him some revenue passed to Glasgow University. When the Trongate was lengthened the new section of street was initially known as the Westergate, but the name was changed to Argyle Street after the funeral cortege of the 4th Duke of Argyll proceeded along it.

This prominent domed structure on Trongate near Glasgow Cross formed part of Glasgow Cross Station, designed by Sir John J. Burnet in 1896 for the Glasgow Central Railway (later absorbed into the Caledonian Railway). Although the station closed in 1964, its low-level tracks are still in use as part of the Argyle Line. Trongate was so important to the city that it was the first street in Glasgow to have a pavement. Flagstones were laid along the front of the Tolbooth, the town chambers and the Tontine Coffee House and these were known as the Plainstanes. A statue of King William of Orange stood in front of these, gifted to the city in 1743 by James Macrae, a Glaswegian who became the Governor of Madras. King Billy was portrayed as a Roman Emperor, wearing a toga and sitting astride a lively horse.

In 1725 the Trongate was the location of the Malt Tax Riot. As a result of wars abroad and insurrection at home, the English malt tax was introduced in Scotland. This increased the price of ale, and the local MP, Campbell of Shawfield, became a target for abuse as he had voted for the tax. A mob ransacked the MP's mansion, which was situated at the corner of Trongate and Glassford Street. Campbell and his family had gone to their country residence a few days beforehand, and in the battle between infantry and townspeople nine citizens were killed and seventeen wounded. The Government was so alarmed that General Wade was despatched with a force consisting of Deloraine's regiment of foot, six troops of the Royal Dragoons, one troop of the Earl of Stair's Dragoons, a company of Highlanders and one gun.

Gardner's Warehouse on Jamaica Street, seen here in 1960, was designed by R. McConnell and built using the cast-iron framed technology employed for the Crystal Palace in London. This enabled the use of large windows with delicate frames, and at the time of its construction in 1856 represented cutting-edge building techniques. It is believed to be the first general purpose cast iron building to be erected in the country. Gardner's were involved in the furniture trade from 1832, but after trading successfully for more than 150 years were acquired by their Edinburgh rivals, Martin & Frost, in 1985. In 2000 the building was extensively refurbished and opened as a bar/restaurant. Jamaica Street was officially opened in 1763 and was named in recognition of the trade between Glasgow and the West Indies. In the late nineteenth century it was known for the large number of warehouses along it.

This picture and the accompanying one – both looking along Argyle Street from Jamaica Street – were taken in 1905 and 1930 respectively. Simpson's Corner, on the right, is named after Robert Simpson who opened a shawl warehouse in the Trongate in 1825 and transferred his business to Jamaica Street in 1851. The shop was gradually extended until it occupied the entire corner, later becoming Arnott Simpson Ltd. Opposite Simpson's was the Adelphi Hotel, originally the Argyle. The Adelphi was owned by the Dunlop family who were in the theatre business. It later incorporated a branch of Boots the Chemist on the ground floor, advertising 'Open Day and Night'. Eventually the hotel was demolished and replaced (as seen on the facing page), at which point Boots took over the entire corner.

Further east along Argyle Street, where the flag is flying on the right, was John Anderson's Royal Polytechnic. This began as a drapery store in the Gorbals in 1837, moved to Jamaica Street, and later relocated to this site on Argyle Street between Dunlop and Maxwell Streets. In 1925 Anderson's son sold out to Lewis's, and by 1935 they had built a new store on the same site – the largest provincial department store in Great Britain. This remained the case until the 1970s when the company built an even larger store in Newcastle-upon-Tyne. The Argyle Street shop has now been incorporated into the St Enoch Shopping Centre and is a branch of Debenhams. According to Ward, Lock & Co.'s *Guide to Glasgow*, published between the wars, Argyle Street was 'always crowded, and on Saturday afternoons and evenings, when the working classes are free from toil, the sea of motley human beings [flows] over the roadway, impeding the vehicular traffic'.

The famous clothing store of Paisley's stood at the corner of the Broomielaw and Jamaica Street. Not only did it stock an extensive range of formal and informal wear, but it also had a large variety of clothes for the merchant service. Many school pupils were taken to Paisley's to buy their new uniforms and had to stand in the blistering heat of summer trying on woollen blazers, hats and scarves! Tram 688 is seen making its way over Glasgow Bridge in this 1914 photograph – it remained in service until 1950. The stores on the right-hand side of the street were demolished to make way for the Royal Stuart Hotel. This subsequently became halls of residence for Strathclyde University.

43

These two photographs, taken c.1894 and 1924, show the second Glasgow Bridge (more commonly known as Jamaica Bridge) before and after the completion of widening work. The original bridge was proposed by the city magistrates and the Merchants' House as part of a joint scheme to extend the town, and the foundation stone was laid in 1767 by Provost George Murdoch. The bridge was built by John Adam of Glasgow at a cost of approximately £9,000, and the opening ceremony featured a procession which left from the Saracen's Head in Gallowgate. The new bridge dated from 1833 and was designed by Thomas Telford, with the foundation stone laid by Hon James Ewing, Lord Provost of Glasgow, in front of a crowd of 50,000. Between 1894 and 1899 the bridge was widened by twenty feet by the architects Cunningham, Blyth & Westland. They reused Telford's original granite facings and balustrades, so the widened bridge does not look substantially different from its narrower predecessor. The temporary structure on the right of the upper picture was put in place as the bridge was widened.

Jamaica Bridge, 1936. In the two previous pictures the landing stage for the Cluthas can just be seen at the north end of the bridge adjacent to Paisley's. Cluthas derived their name from the Gaelic word for the Clyde. Twelve of them were introduced in 1884 and they ran from Stockwell Street Bridge to eleven landing stages between there and Whiteinch, three and a half miles away. The journey took 45 minutes and the fare was a penny. In 1891 the Cluthas carried 3,500,000 passengers, but were withdrawn in 1903. The iron girder railway bridge seen here leads in and out of Central Station, which was opened by the Caledonian Railway in 1879 and extended in 1890 and 1906. The Glasgow & South Western Railway had refused to allow the Caledonian rights to its St Enoch Station, so it had to buy property all the way up Bridge Street, Alston Street and Gordon Street in order to build its own terminus. Following the railway grouping of 1923, the station became the mainline terminus for the London, Midland & Scottish Railway's services to London and Birmingham.

This photograph of the Clyde was taken from the Glasgow Sailors' Home. Proposals for a sailors' hostel in the Broomielaw were first mooted in 1853, and in 1855–6 a building was erected at 150 Broomielaw at a cost of £12,000. This featured a square tower at one corner and a circular campanile on the corner of James Watt Street. As part of major reconstruction work another floor was added in 1906. After the Second World War shipping declined in Glasgow and in 1971 the home was demolished. The domed building on the left belongs to the Clyde Port Authority (formerly the Clyde Navigation Trust) building in Robertson Street. Established in 1858, the Trust had extensive powers and built an appropriately ornate building as its headquarters (constructed in two stages between 1882 and 1908). Two ships' prows, complete with anchors, flank the main entrance, and there is an image of Poseidon on a pediment supported by four columns. There are also statues of Thomas Telford, James Watt and Henry Bell, while a plaque displays the Trust's symbol of a lighthouse.

George Square originally formed part of a croft called Ramshorn, and in 1609 became the property of George Hutcheson, the founder of Hutcheson's Hospital. It was leased by the patrons of the hospital to small crofters and gardeners, although in 1703 the former asked for a rent abatement because of the 'barrenness of the ground'. In 1772 the area began to acquire value for building purposes, and the city magistrates purchased the lands of Ramshorn and Meadowflats. George Square was laid out in 1781, although this involved little more than marking the boundaries. Twenty years later a writer described it as 'a hollow, filled with green-water, and a favourite resort for drowning puppies and cats and dogs, while the banks of this suburban pool [are] the slaughtering place of horses'. A caricature of the square dating from 1825 shows children playing and women washing clothes. For a while a railing surrounded the square, but this was removed in 1876 and not replaced. The pedimented building on the right of this 1870 picture (looking east) incorporated the George Hotel at its right-hand end. The whole of the east side of the square subsequently became the site of the City Chambers.

The Merchants' House, with its ship weathervane, was built on the western side of the square in 1889 to the designs of John J. Burnet. It stands on the site of the Globe and Clarence Hotels, while the Bank of Scotland opened premises on the same side of the square in 1872, demolishing the Waverley and Crow Hotels to do so. The latter were the original ventures of the Cranston family. When this nineteenth century photograph was taken the western side of George Square incorporated four hotels. From left to right these were the Waverley, Crow, Clarence and Globe.

Looking north-west across George Square towards Queen Street Station, the roof of which is visible in the background. This c.1870 photograph was taken from the south side of the square, which subsequently became the site of the General Post Office. The Prince of Wales laid the foundation stone of this enormous building on 17 October 1876, and 8,000 Freemasons from all over Scotland attended the ceremony. Until the introduction of the London mail coach, all items going south were taken by a Newcastle wagon, drawn by eight horses, and mail took a minimum of eighteen days to complete the journey to London. The development of the national rail network slashed the time taken to transport mail across the country.

When the site of the George Hotel was required for Glasgow's new municipal buildings (the City Chambers), the hotel relocated to the north side of the Square and became the North British Station Hotel. This establishment also incorporated the old Queen's and Wellington Hotels, and another storey was added later. The Royal Hotel was also on the northern side of the square and can be seen in the upper picture on the facing page. This view of the north side of the square shows the Queen's Hotel.

George Square was named after King George III and was meant to have his statue at its centre. However, the column in the middle bears a statue of Sir Walter Scott, erected in 1837. The City Chambers were opened on 22 August 1888 by Queen Victoria, having been designed by William Young and built by Messrs Morrison & Mason. Prior to their opening, a number of other buildings had been used for civic purposes. New chambers were built fronting Ingram Street in 1874, but a competition was then launched for replacement buildings in George Square. The City Chambers' entrance is based on the third-century Arch of Constantine in Rome, and the hall is in the shape of a Renaissance Roman church. The owners of the Queen Anne restaurant in Glasgow allegedly served a ton of Welsh rarebit (a dish that they had apparently introduced to Glasgow!) at the opening of the City Chambers. The white granite cenotaph in the centre of the picture was designed by J. J. Burnet to commemorate the 18,000 men from Glasgow who died in the First World War.

The origins of Buchanan Street can be traced to 15 February 1763 when Andrew Buchanan purchased five acres of land with the intention of laying out a street of grand buildings. When the American War of Independence intervened he lost his trading company and the bank took over, starting to sell steadings in Buchanan Street the following year. By 1780 it had been laid out as far as Gordon Street and had been completed up to Port Dundas by 1804. In the early days it mainly featured villas and farms, with the occasional workshop. The church in the middle distance is St George's Tron of 1807–12. It was the first great building in the street, and was designed by William Stark. The first commercial enterprise came to Buchanan Street in 1828 when the Argyle Arcade was built. According to Ward, Lock & Co.'s inter-war guide to Glasgow, 'While the "masses" take their pleasure in Argyle Street the "classes" enjoy their afternoon promenade in Buchanan Street'. On the right of this c.1870 photograph is the Waverley Temperance Hotel, later the Ivanhoe, and now the Buchanan Hotel. The spire of St Enoch's Church is in the distance.

In 1847 the Glasgow Assembly Rooms in Ingram Street were rented to provide 'a literary and scientific institution adapted to the wants of the commercial classes of Glasgow'. The formal opening of the Glasgow Athenaeum took place in the City Hall at a large meeting presided over by Charles Dickens. In 1888 the institution moved into buildings in St George's Place which were opened by the Marquess of Bute. Courses were available in mercantile law, political economy, commercial geography, modern history, English literature, French, German and Spanish. By 1901 2,500 students had enrolled, and in 1890 a school of music was organised on the lines of the Continental conservatoires. The first meeting of the Old Glasgow Club was held in the building in 1900. The Athenaeum Theatre at 179 Buchanan Street (illustrated here) was designed by J. J. Burnet and built between 1891 and 1893. It had a long association with amateur dramatic clubs, some of which had been connected to the Athenaeum. In the 1940s it became the temporary home of the Glasgow Unity Theatre and the Glasgow Citizens' company, which staged its first performance of James Bridie's *Holy Isle* there in 1943. Along with Dr Honeyman, a director of Glasgow Art Galleries, and George Singleton, owner of the Cosmo Cinema, Bridie formed the Glasgow Citizens' company.

In 1783 the Royal Bank of Scotland opened its first branch in Glasgow, the joint agents being David Dale and Robert Scott-Moncrieff. The bank was originally located in Hopkirk's Land near Glasgow Cross: it occupied half of David Dale's linen shop and the bank paid him rent of £2.10s. In 1798 the Royal Bank moved to new premises in St Andrew's Square, and then in 1817 purchased William Cunninghame's former mansion facing Queen Street in what later became Royal Exchange Square. The directors of the bank sold the mansion in 1827 and bought another, this time fronting on to Buchanan Street. Customers included 'maltmen, tallow chandlers, hucksters, glewmakers, qualifiers of tobacco, lint-hecklers, change-keepers, inkle manufacturers, and pocket-book makers'. This picture shows the additions made to the Buchanan Street facade by Charles Wilson in 1850–1.

The Glasgow Stock Exchange was instituted in July 1844 with 28 members. No dealing in shares was known in Glasgow until 1830, when Sir James Watson began business as a stockbroker. The first meeting of the exchange was at 3 North Exchange Court, after which it moved to St George's Place. In 1847 the members transferred to the National Bank Buildings, but the premises there became too cramped and this new building was erected in Buchanan Street in 1874. It was designed by J. J. Burnet, who added extensions in 1903–4, utilising space in St George's Place (now Nelson Mandela Place). The doorway in Buchanan Street has an arched canopy with carved representations of different races of the world: European, African, Indian and Chinese. With the exception of the facade the whole building was rebuilt between 1969 and 1971.

This interior view of the stock exchange dates from 1955.

In the early 1950s horse-drawn traffic was banned from Buchanan Street, although the ban didn't extend to mounted police who are still sometimes seen in the street today. The former offices of George Outram & Co. stand on the west side of the street, marked by statues of Caxton and Gutenberg at the doorway. At one time the company published three daily newspapers: the *Glasgow Herald*, the *Bulletin* and the *Evening Times*. In 1980 they moved their premises to Albion Street. The series of buildings now occupied by Fraser's are an amalgam of four former shops: Wylie & Lochhead's, Macdonald's, Kemp's Shawl Emporium and Maclure & Macdonald. The sign for one of Miss Cranston's tea rooms is on the right. Behind the policeman and out of sight is the entrance to Argyle Arcade. This contained the first shop in the city to have plate glass windows. Possibly the best remembered business in the arcade was the Clyde Model Dockyard, established in 1789 and selling model cars, yachts and trains. Today most of the shops are jewellers. Just opposite the entrance to the arcade was the Buchanan Street Hotel. It had a walled garden with fruit trees and a large conservatory where grapes were grown. This photograph was taken in 1926.

The original Fraser & Sons shop was opened on the east side of Buchanan Street in 1873. This photograph and the one opposite, both taken in 1948, show just how congested the street had become in the days when two-way traffic flowed along it. The street has now been pedestrianised and relaid with granite setts.

Looking south along Buchanan Street. Cook's Travel Office (right) was part of Thomas Cook & Sons, once the sole travel agency in the city. The Clydesdale Bank sign marks the site of another building once owned by Miss Cranston. Its furnishings were designed by George Walton and it contained a large mural by Charles Rennie Mackintosh.

St Enoch Square was originally lined with mansion houses and laid out with grass. Later a church was built in the centre. Opened in 1876, St Enoch Station was designed by Sir John Fowler and J. F. Blair and based on St Pancras Station in London, although on a much smaller scale. St Enoch was the terminus of the Glasgow & South Western Railway, and the first major railway bridge to be built across the river led into it. In the early 1900s six extra platforms were added to the south side. The St Enoch Hotel was opened in 1880 to designs by Thomas Wilson, a church architect from Hampstead. In 1966 the station closed and the St Enoch Shopping Centre now stands in its place. Parliament approved plans for an underground cable railway in Glasgow in 1890, and although most subway stations were entered through a tenement, James Miller was commissioned to provide a suitable building for St Enoch Square. Seen on the right, it is now used as a travel information centre.

The Mitchell family made their fortune through tobacco, and when Stephen Mitchell died a bachelor in 1874 he left most of his fortune of £66,998.10s.6d. to 'form the nucleus of a fund for the establishment and endowment of a large public library in Glasgow'. No one was to be excluded from using the library and no books were to be banned, even if they challenged current opinions on politics and religion. In 1877 the Mitchell Library opened in temporary premises in Ingram Street, illustrated here. As its stock increased it relocated to 21 Miller Street in 1891. More and more books were added to the collection, many of them valuable, and a competition to design new premises was won by Glasgow architect W. B. Whitie. Andrew Carnegie laid the memorial stone in 1907, and by 1911 the new Mitchell Library had opened. An extension was started in 1939 and finally completed in 1963. After St Andrew's Halls burnt down in 1962 a further addition to the library was planned, and this opened in 1982.

The building that later became known as the Royal Exchange was built at a cost of £10,000 as a private house c.1778 for William Cunninghame, one of the Tobacco Lords of Glasgow, and was considered 'one of the most splendid houses then built in the West of Scotland'. In 1789 John Stirling purchased the property, and in 1817 his sons sold it to the Royal Bank of Scotland. The bank in turn sold the mansion to a consortium of city merchants, manufacturers and magistrates in 1827, in order that an 'exchange' be built. David Hamilton was commissioned to incorporate the old mansion house into the Exchange, and its foundation stone was laid in December 1827. The building included a reading room, exhibition room, newsroom, underwriters' rooms, bankers' offices, and sugar, cotton and other rooms for samples of goods. The Exchange's committee was uncompromising in its decisions about what the new buildings on the north and south sides should be used for. Nothing 'offensive' was to be sold, such as vegetables or cheese!

After the Second World War the City of Glasgow bought the Royal Exchange for £105,000, and in 1949 the Stirling Library moved into it from Miller Street. The library was named after Walter Stirling, who had left his collection of books to the city in 1791. In 1994 the library returned to Miller Street and the building was converted into the city's Gallery of Modern Art.

Spacious St Vincent Place, seen here in 1914, was designed as a terminus for horse-drawn carriages. There were many commercial premises in the street, including those of the *Citizen*, where a number of prominent Glasgow publications were produced. The *Glasgow Citizen* was first published in 1842 and changed its name several times prior to ceasing publication in 1974. The building on the left was built in 1870 for the Clydesdale Bank, while the Bank of Scotland building further down the street opened in 1869. In January 1892 a gents public toilet was opened here, as indicated by the railings on the right. This had five urinal stalls, four WCs, two wash-hand basins and an attendant's room. Customers were charged for the privilege of using the toilets and in May 1912 the annual income generated was recorded as £157.17*s*.5*d*. The following year the toilets were lit by electricity and extended.

The land on which Gordon Street was laid out belonged to Alexander 'Picture' Gordon. He built a large house in Buchanan Street c.1804, opposite what is now Gordon Street, and purchased the land there so that his views would remain unrestricted. The south side of the street was built up c.1815 and the rest was developed between 1850 and 1890. On the right is the cast-iron canopy of Central Station. The station was built between 1876 and 1879 by the Caledonian Railway as the Glasgow terminus for its southern services. It was later extended to provide thirteen platforms. Above the station is the Central Hotel, originally built as the Caledonian Railway's headquarters. On the left is the Grosvenor building, with the Renfield Street junction in the centre. Forsyth's outfitters stood at this corner. Its premises were originally designed as a warehouse in 1858, but were converted to a shop in 1908 by J. J. Burnet. This photograph dates from 1914.

The building housing the Grosvenor restaurant in Gordon Street was designed and owned by Alexander and George Thomson, and was opened in the early 1860s. At that time it had four storeys and a basement. In the late 1890s the ground and first floors were taken over as a restaurant by William McKillop, who made a series of alterations. He designed a new street-level frontage and reconstructed the interior, adding a grand staircase leading to the upper floor. In 1902 plans were approved for an additional two storeys to be built on top of the existing building and the second and third floors of the original structure were turned into a grand hall suitable for banquets, dances or large functions. The marble staircase was extended and adorned with sculpted figures and stained glass. In the dining hall structural steelwork was hidden behind ornate plaster and woodwork, designed by J. H. Craigie of Clarke & Bell. When large functions began to wane in popularity the restaurant closed and after a serious fire the building was turned into offices. No hint of the earlier spectacular interiors remain.

Forsyth's building is on the left of this 1936 view of Renfield Street. Above the name of the store is a figure of a woman shrouded in a cloak, and above her are cherubs representing Britain and India. There are also sculptures depicting Canada, Australia and Africa. On the other side of the street are Austin Reed's and Reid & Todd's. The Paramount Cinema, further up the street on the right, opened on Hogmanay 1934 and could seat 2,800 patrons. In 1954, after it had been taken over by Oscar Deutsch, 50,000 people went to see *The Robe* there in its first week. The building also had full stage facilities and many entertainers performed there in the 1950s and 60s, including the Beatles and the Rolling Stones. In 1969 the Rank organisation subdivided the cinema to make room for three screens. It reopened in 1970 with *Cromwell*, *Airport* and *The Virgin and the Gypsy*.

The original name of Hope Street (seen here in 1962) was Copenhagen Street. The building in the foreground has been demolished, but the one beyond it, displaying the sign 'Record House', survives. This was the former *Glasgow Evening News* offices. One of the doorways features two cherubs reading from a book, with two owls looking on. In the 1920s the *Daily Record* moved here from premises in Renfield Street and both newspapers were then published from the Hope Street building. The printing works were built next door between 1933 and 1937. On the left is the vehicular entrance to Central Station, which handcarts, horse-drawn and slow-moving vehicles were apparently not allowed to use.

Charing Cross, 1949.

Chapter 4
Sauchiehall Street to the West End

In the early nineteenth century the first tentative attempts to develop an upmarket residential suburb in the city's West End were made by James Gibson when he started to feu his lands of Hillhead. The New Anniesland Turnpike Act of 1836 acted as a catalyst for this process, paving the way for a new road and high-level bridge over the River Kelvin and making the planned suburbs readily accessible from the city centre. Previously they had been considered undesirably far away and difficult to reach.

A gradual shift of important institutions to the embryonic West End helped encourage further residential development. The Botanic Gardens at Kelvinside was one such institution, opening in spring 1842 soon after completion of the new turnpike road. The gardens had their origins in the Physic Gardens associated with the Old College in High Street, and in 1845 this too established its first link with the West End when it formally took over the observatory on Dowanhill which had been privately financed and opened in 1842. Railway development in the city centre gave the Old College the opportunity to sell its cramped High Street site at a premium and relocate to a spacious new campus. It purchased Gilmorehill House and its 43

acres of land in the West End in the 1860s, along with a further nineteen acres from adjoining estates. The concurrent development of other West End institutions such as Kelvingrove Park and Gartnavel Hospital, combined with continued improvements to transport links, led to a process of urban development that saw the West End grow and expand.

Sauchiehall Street formed an important thoroughfare from the city centre to the West End, making the transition from a residential street to one of Glasgow's most popular shopping districts as the commercial centre spread west. Over a period of 150 years T. & R. Annan & Sons has traded from four locations on Sauchiehall Street, with the company's flagship premises at No. 518 remaining its home for 55 years.

The photographs in this chapter show a wide variety of locations, from a Sauchiehall Street thronged with shoppers to the open spaces of Kelvingrove Park and its two International Exhibitions. There are also views of the university, the Kelvin and its mills, and the once independent Burgh of Partick. Three less well-known locations at the end of the chapter illustrate areas that have now changed beyond recognition.

Sauchiehall Street's name derives from the Gaelic *sauchie-haugh* – the meadow (*haugh*) of the willow trees (*sauch*). Until 1807 it was nothing more than a winding lane from Clayslaps at Kelvingrove to the top of Buchanan Street. Villas were gradually built, followed by several terraces of houses. In 1846 this winding thoroughfare was straightened and transformed into an impressive street 60 feet wide between Buchanan Street and Charing Cross, and extended to connect with Dumbarton Road in 1855. The houses eventually gave way to shops as the city centre moved westwards. The 'Piccadilly' sign above Lumley House advertises what was then Glasgow's only nightclub, opened in 1927, the year before this picture was taken. It replaced the Picture Salon that was established on the site in 1914.

Opposite: The building on the right of this 1900 picture stood at 140 Sauchiehall Street and belonged to Messrs Cumming & Smith, who described themselves – not very snappily – as 'wholesale upholsterers, furnishers, cabinet, chair, sofa frame, bedding manufacturers, complete house furnishers, carpet factors, removal contractors etc.'. The company had begun business in North Wallace Street, Townhead, in the mid-1870s. The Sauchiehall Street building was designed by H. & D. Barclay and put up as showrooms and warehouses in 1892–3 at a cost of £35,000. By 1903 the company had returned to Townhead. The site is now occupied by part of the Savoy Centre, which takes its name from the Savoy Cinema that stood nearby.

Sauchiehall Street looking west from Hope Street, 1949. On the left beyond tram No. 50 is the frontage of Glasgow's La Scala cinema. This was opened in October 1912 and was famous for its tea room in the main stalls. Lunch and tea was served there until the 1950s when the tea room closed. The cinema also boasted a British Christie Unit Organ – 'one of the most modern music marvels'. Across the road from La Scala was the Gaumont Picture House. This had opened in 1910 as the Picture House. It was renamed the Gaumont in 1948 (a year before this picture was taken) and specialised in running epic films. Most of these lasted about three hours and to maximise profits advance bookings were taken with special prices offered. The first film to be screened under this system was *The Ten Commandments*: it began showing on 26 May 1958 and ran for four months. *South Pacific* followed with a run of eighteen months. *The Sound of Music* arrived on 16 April 1965 and finally closed on 23 December 1967, a record that has never been exceeded. James Craig's Rhul Restaurant was noted for its Scottish paintings, which were sold off cheaply when the restaurant closed in the 1950s. By 1965 one-way traffic had been introduced along Sauchiehall Street.

Tram 226 approaches the corner of Hope Street as it travels along Sauchiehall Street on its way to Dumbreck in 1922. Watt Brothers' department store still occupies the site on the left. The business began as the Ribbon Shop in Elmbank Street and moved to its present location in 1915.

This early view of Sauchiehall Street looks west towards Charing Cross in the years before the northern side of the street was built up. In those days the gardens of some Renfrew Street properties sloped right down to Sauchiehall Street. The nearer spire belongs to Renfield St Stephen's Church. The spire beyond it is what is now the Henry Wood Hall, home of the Royal Scottish National Orchestra since 1978. Designed by John Honeyman, it opened as Trinity Congregational Church in 1864. In the distance on the right is the tower of Charles Wilson's Trinity College, built for the Free Church of Scotland. The building was badly affected by a fire in 1903 and was later rebuilt as a library. Today it is apartments and offices.

Pettigrew & Stephens vied with Copeland & Lye for the title of Sauchiehall Street's favourite department store. Their shop, Manchester House, was opened under the guidance of Andrew Pettigrew who eventually became sole proprietor. As the business grew it took over Bath Street's Alexandria Hotel and the former Glasgow Institute of Fine Arts, seen here on the left. This had its origins in the Dilettanti Society, founded in 1825. Although this was disbanded after 1838 a new institution grew from it: the West of Scotland Academy. The body that succeeded this – the Institute of Fine Arts – began exhibiting in 1861 and by 1880 had a permanent home in Sauchiehall Street, designed by J. J. Burnet. Having become part of Pettigrew & Stephens, this was destroyed by fire in 1963, and in the 1970s the whole of the former shop was demolished to make way for the Sauchiehall Street Centre. Pettigrew & Stephens' rivals Copeland's opened their 'Caledonian House' in 1878, having begun trading in Cowcaddens in 1873. Caledonian House was described as 'one of the most extensive, most architecturally elegant and most perfectly equipped drapery emporiums to be met with in the Kingdom'.

This 1934 photograph of Sauchiehall Street shows Cuthbertson's music shop on the left, with Daly's department store to the right. This building had previously housed Miss Cranston's Willow Tea Rooms, which under different ownership subsequently became the Kensington. Many of the interiors were destroyed when Daly's took over the building, although the Salon de Luxe survived and was restored in 1974. On the left along this stretch of the street was Reid & Todd's, which sold 'umbrellas, waterproofs, ladies' sportswear and swimwear, fancy leather goods, trunks and travelling requisites'. Further east was Muirhead's department store, part of the Fraser empire.

Designed by Alexander 'Greek' Thomson, this building at 336–56 Sauchiehall Street dates from 1865. It is unusual for Thomson because it is built on a corner site, rather than as part of a terrace, and consequently allowed him to continue his designs into Scott Street. The influences are a mixture of Greek and Egyptian, and the building is now used as the Centre for Contemporary Arts having been extensively refurbished in the 1990s.

The building on the left with the winged statue above its facade began as the Vitagraph in 1912, then became the King's Cinema in 1938. In the summer patrons could sit outside on the small balcony above the entrance. Because it was so narrow, the cinema auditorium was only eight seats wide. Nearer the camera are premises that were designed for T. & R. Annan by the architectural practice of John Honeyman, Keppie & Mackintosh. They are now used as the Royal Highland Fusiliers regimental museum. The Locarno, in the foreground, was one of Glasgow's many dance halls. It opened in 1926, and by 1927 the *Evening Times* was reporting that 'Sauchiehall Street blossoms with dancing-palaces that vie in size with the greatest cinema houses and incorporate features like garages, tea rooms, lounges, and club rooms'. The Locarno later changed its name to Tiffany's before becoming a casino in 1989.

Opposite: The fountain just visible on the left beside the post office was erected by public subscription in memory of Sir James Cameron. He was best known for his involvement in the Abolition of Imprisonment for Debt Act in Scotland, and also sponsored the bill that became the Cremation Act in 1902, making cremation a legal alternative to burial. The Grand Hotel (left) was erected between 1875 and 1878 by John Duncanson, but when the big railway companies built their own large hotels next to railway stations its popularity diminished as it was too far from the main stations. During the Second World War it was taken over by the American Red Cross as their Comforts Club for US forces on leave. In 1968 the Grand was demolished and the rubble used to infill the dry dock at Meadowside.

Charing Cross Mansions (left) were built between 1889 and 1891 to designs by Burnet, Son, & Campbell. The baroque clock is surrounded by carved figures designed by the sculptor William Birnie Rhind. One of R. S. McColl's newsagents is in the foreground of this 1938 photograph. Robert Smythe McColl was a famous footballer as well as the co-founder of the R. S. McColl chain. He first played for Queen's Park in 1893 before transferring to Newcastle United and Glasgow Rangers, and was also capped fifteen times for Scotland. On the opposite corner where the crowd is standing are William Skinner's tea rooms. Founded in 1835, these were as popular as Craig's or Cranston's, surviving until 1961. Soon after this photograph was taken the Beresford Hotel (visible in the picture on page 60) opened on Sauchiehall Street near Charing Cross. This art deco landmark attracted many visitors to the 1938 Empire Exhibition in Bellahouston and was originally decorated with red, black and mustard-coloured tiles, complementing the style of many of the exhibition's buildings.

Sir George Gilbert Scott (1810–77) was the architect of the University of Glasgow's new building at Gilmorehill in the West End, and on 8 October 1868 the Prince and Princess of Wales laid the foundation stone of the dramatic new structure in front of 20,000 spectators. It was opened for use (albeit incomplete) in summer 1870, with the last meeting of the senate of the Old College in High Street taking place in July. The first parts of the new building to be finished were the lecture theatres, offices, laboratories, library and museum. The Bute and Randolph Halls were only completed in 1882 with the aid of generous bequests from the Marquess of Bute and Charles Randolph. Largely to gain the benefit of the scaffolding that was put in place for the lower storeys, the tower was built to its full height of 192 feet at the outset, but it was not until 1888 that a bequest by Andrew Cunningham allowed the addition of the spire (designed by Gilbert Scott's son, J. Oldrid Scott), and a clock with chimes.

This view looking north-west from the university tower was taken in 1937, prior to the rapid expansion of the campus in the 1960s. University Gardens is in the centre, with Lilybank House behind it, shrouded by trees. John Blackie of the Blackie publishing empire formerly lived in the house and commissioned Alexander 'Greek' Thomson to extend it in 1863. The steep slate roof of what was Belmont Church (now part of Hutchesons' Grammar School) in Great George Street is in the centre. The steeple of Kelvinside Parish Church at the top of Byres Road is visible at the top right of the photograph, with Kelvinside Hillhead Parish Church to its left. Opened in 1876, the latter was designed by James Sellars and is modelled on Sainte Chapelle in Paris. In the left foreground are some of the buildings in Professors' Square. These tall villas were originally designed to house academics, although many of the buildings have since been taken over by departments. The Principal's residence is at the southern end of the square. Lord Kelvin occupied No. 11 and a plaque beside the door bears the legend: 'In this house lived William Thomson, Lord Kelvin. Physicist 1824–1907. He matriculated in the university at the age of 10, was its professor of natural philosophy from 1846–1899, and died as its chancellor. He is buried beside Isaac Newton in Westminster Abbey.'

Glasgow's municipal museums and galleries were founded in 1854 when a collection of paintings was bequeathed to the city by Archibald McLellan, along with a building (the McLellan Galleries) to display them in. The Corporation subsequently purchased the small mansion of Kelvingrove House to display objects of scientific and historical interest, but it was felt that a new building was needed to house all the exhibits under one roof. A competition was launched for the design of this new building, with the winning entry submitted by John W. Simpson and E. J. Milner Allen. In 1896 the original promoters ran out of money and the project was handed over to Glasgow Corporation. Kelvingrove Museum and Art Gallery was opened in 1901 by Princess Louise, Duchess of Fife, having cost £250,000. In the centre right of this picture is the Van Houten's tea room, built for the 1901 International Exhibition and located near the rockery bandstand. It offered a serviette, biscuit and Royal Worcester cup of cocoa for the grand sum of one penny! When this 1904 photograph was taken sheep were being used to keep the grass tidy in part of the park.

This 1928 photograph shows Kelvingrove Museum and Art Gallery's central hall with its display of statuary. The pillars in the hall are decorated with the names and badges of Glasgow's fourteen trades: hammermen (engineers), tailors, cordiners (bootmakers), maltmen (brewers), weavers, bakers, skinners, wrights (metalworkers), coopers, fleshers (butchers), masons, gardeners, barbers and bonnetmakers & dyers. The magnificent Lewis pipe organ at the north end of the hall had originally been a feature of the concert hall at the 1901 Exhibition.

The land on which Kelvingrove Park (also known as the West End Park) was laid out was acquired in 1852. In order to form the park, the town council bought the lands of Kelvingrove and Woodlands, with some adjoining portions of Claremont, Woodside and Blythswood, at a cost of £77,995. The crest of the hill and the slopes towards Woodlands were reserved for feuing, and are now the site of Park Terrace, Park Quadrant, Park Circus and Park Gardens. The right was also reserved to feu a strip 120 feet in depth fronting Royal Terrace and Park Grove Terrace. 45 acres were laid out in perpetuity as a public park from designs by Sir Joseph Paxton, and over the next 30 years Kelvingrove Park was expanded. Initially there was very vocal criticism of the lack of space for games, with many people regarding it more as a large garden than a place of recreation. However, with the addition of bowling greens, tennis courts and a bandstand this shortcoming was rectified.

This 1905 view from the university tower looks west-south-west across the city. The chimney on the left belonged to a refuse incinerator. Neither Yorkhill Hospital nor the Kelvin Hall had been built when the photograph was taken. On the Kelvin, to the right of centre, are the Regent and Scotstoun Mills, while in the right foreground the university's West Medical Building is under construction.

This 1937 photograph contrasts with the previous one and illustrates the development of the West End over a 30-year period. The original Kelvin Hall had been destroyed by fire on 7 July 1925 and its replacement (below) opened two years later. The new Kelvin Hall boasted 170,000 square feet of exhibition space and was used for numerous trade fairs, as well as the annual Christmas carnival and circus. During the Second World War it was converted into the country's chief factory for the manufacture of barrage and convoy balloons. The Royal Hospital for Sick Children at Yorkhill is in the left background, and to its right a ship can be seen at Yorkhill

Quay. In 1940 a bomb set fire to the cruiser *Sussex* at Yorkhill and the hospital had to be evacuated because of the possibility that the ship's magazine might blow up. The Royal Hospital for Sick Children was founded in 1883 in Scott Street and moved to Yorkhill in 1916. The first building there became dangerous and had to be demolished in 1965, with services relocated to Oakbank Hospital until a replacement could be built. The present hospital was constructed between 1968 and 1971. On the far right is the 1914 part of the Meadowside Granary complex: the next section was being constructed at the time the photograph was taken.

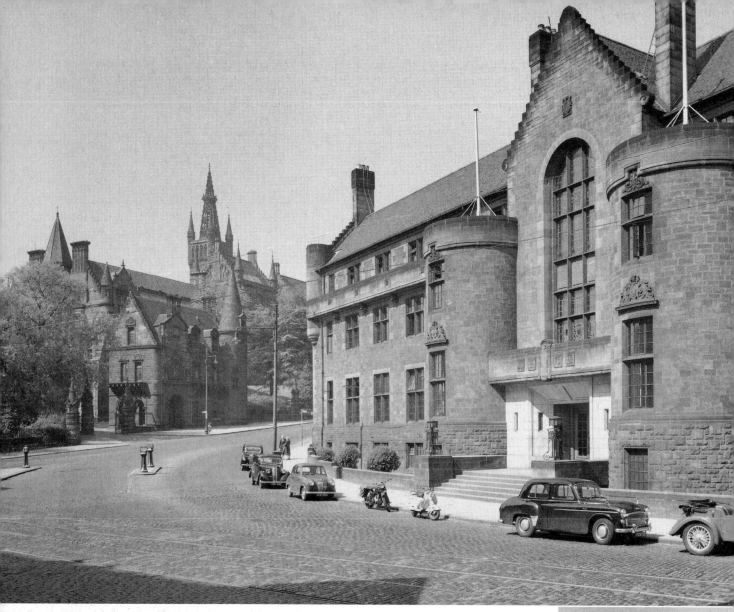

When the university moved to Gilmorehill there was a distinct lack of social facilities for the students. A meeting was held in the Bute Hall in 1885 and plans for a union, vigorously encouraged by Principal John Caird, rapidly took shape. Dr John MacIntyre made a generous donation, the students themselves held a great bazaar in 1889, and the university court gave financial assistance, with the result that the Men's Union was formally opened in 1890. It now houses a book shop and the Students' Representative Council. The Women's Union came into being at roughly the same time, with a new Mens' Union (seen here) built between 1929 and 1931 on University Avenue near the junction with Gibson Street. It has a relief sculpture of St Mungo above the doorway, with Glasgow University's badge high up on the gable. The union is well known for its debates, the infamous basement Beer Bar and its snooker hall, though not necessarily in that order. To the left is Pearce Lodge, named after Sir William Pearce, a wealthy shipbuilder and MP for Govan. The building is of great historical importance as part of it was moved and rebuilt from the seventeenth century Old College. The original sections (dating from 1656) include the gateway facing University Avenue, the cornice and the coat of arms. When first reconstructed c.1888, the building was used as the naval architecture classroom.

Although proposals to build a teaching hospital were put forward by Glasgow University Court as early as 1845, it was not until the university moved to Gilmorehill that plans were actually drawn up. John Burnet was appointed as architect on 26 June 1867, and his designs were submitted two years later. It had become clear by then that – apart from the university's requirements – the hospital would have to serve as a second infirmary for the city. In 1871 the Lord Provost of Glasgow convened a committee to promote and erect a new hospital to be called the Western Infirmary. Work began that year and the building opened in October 1874, with the first inpatients admitted on 2 November. Within a couple of days two medical and two surgical wards were completely filled, with 110 inpatients admitted by the end of November. In 1898 money was raised to commemorate Charles Lutwidge Dodgson (Lewis Carroll) and an 'Alice in Wonderland cot' was purchased for £15. The cot remained in Ward 13 for years before eventually disintegrating! From the rest of the money raised, £220 was allocated to looking after child patients at the Western, and in 1898 there were 567 such patients. The gatehouse on the left was recently refurbished and is now the Maggie's Cancer Care Centre. The spire behind it is that of Old Partick Parish Church (now demolished) in Church Street. By 1974 the open ground in the centre of the photograph had been covered by a modern hospital building.

Glasgow staged a series of great exhibitions in 1888, 1901, 1911 and 1938. The 1901 Exhibition was nicknamed 'The Groveries' (perhaps because of its location in Kelvingrove Park) and was the largest such event to have been held in Britain at that time. It was intended to illustrate the growth of art, industry and science during the nineteenth century, and the meeting of the British Association for the Advancement of Science was held in the city the same year. Eleven and a half million visitors came to the exhibition, one of the main attractions being the machinery hall, which stood on the site of the present Kelvin Hall. To provide access to the hall, a 1,000-foot covered walkway was built across Dumbarton Road as part of the 'Grand Avenue'. T. & R. Annan & Sons were official photographers to the 1901 Exhibition, and this picture shows their portrait studio.

The exhibition was made up of temporary buildings, the main one of which was the Eastern Palace, illustrated here with Kelvingrove Museum and Art Gallery – which officially opened on 2 May 1901 – beyond it. The palace was topped with a grand dome featuring an angel of light wielding an electric torch. Many other attractions were constructed for the exhibition including a Russian village; a model farm complete with working dairy, windmill and grieve's house; a grand concert hall to seat over 3,000; and a new sports ground at Gilmorehill with a four-lap cement cycle track, cinder pedestrian course, football pitch and stand accommodation for 25,000 spectators. Many of the venues were lit by electricity at night.

Among the 1901 Exhibition's other attractions were a Canadian water chute that plunged into the Kelvin; gondola trips on the river (illustrated here); a rifle range; and a switchback railway. Lord Kelvin was honorary vice-president of the event, and his new telephone system was on display along with art, historical items and industrial products from all over the world. Sir William Burrell was one of the principal lenders of exhibits and many of his treasures were moved to the new art gallery at the close of the exhibition on 9 November. The event's architect was James Miller, who was responsible for laying out buildings over the 73 acre site. Railway companies encouraged people to attend from all over Britain by offering cheap excursion fares, and Glasgow celebrated by introducing new tram services powered by electricity from the newly opened Pinkston generating station. Even the weather played its part – for once it was good – and such illustrious figures as the Tsar of Russia visited the exhibition.

The purpose of the 1911 Exhibition was to raise funds to found and endow a Chair of Scottish History and Literature at Glasgow University. The exhibition's main architect was R. J. Walker, and there was much evidence of Scots Baronial style. Once again, T. & R. Annan were the official photographers.

The 1911 venture was smaller than that of 1901, but nonetheless had many noteworthy attractions. These included a Highland village, *An Clachan*, seen here with Gilmorehill Halls (previously Gilmorehill Church) in University Avenue in the background. Near the banks of the Kelvin a large stone can still be seen bearing the inscription *An Clachan* and marking the site. All the people working in the village were Gaelic-speaking Highlanders.

There was also an old Scottish town, illustrated here, although the West African village was perhaps more unusual. In addition to these visitors could enjoy an aerial railway, a mountain slide, and ride in motor boats – instead of gondolas – on the Kelvin. A flotilla of model ships was also exhibited on the Kelvin, and elsewhere visitors could even go to see Flora MacDonald's slippers on display!

Many of the buildings were ornate, such as the Palace of Industry, seen here from the music court. Entertainment was laid on by German and Hungarian bands and there were sessions of mass hymn singing. On the final day of the exhibition a huge storm blew the roof off the Aviation Pavilion and up to Park Terrace, and many of the other buildings were severely damaged.

Below: Glasgow's Botanic Gardens were not always in Kelvinside, and had their origins at the Old College in High Street. There were Physic Gardens and a Chair of Anatomy and Botany at the college, but after the founding of a botanical society in 1816 a search began for a bigger site for a botanic garden in the city. Initially eight acres at Sandyford were used, but by the 1830s it had become clear that the gardens were too small. New botanic gardens were opened on their present site in 1842, with many of the plants from Sandyford being transferred. At first the gardens were a private institution, but they were also open to day visitors who were charged a small entrance fee. The Kibble Palace, seen here, had originally been built for John Kibble at Coulport at a cost of approximately £15,000. For reasons that are unclear he first offered the building to Glasgow for erection in Queen's Park, proposing to enlarge the main dome. However, conditions were attached to his offer – that he be allowed to promote functions and charge admission. Initially the council was interested, but after a delay of three months Kibble withdrew his offer and looked instead to the Royal Botanic Institution of Glasgow. This body was struggling financially and saw his offer as a way to overcome their difficulties. The structure at Coulport was dismantled in May 1872 and the first public concert was held in the newly reconstructed (and extended) building on 20 June 1873.

This 1924 picture of Great Western Road shows two churches – St Mary's Episcopal Cathedral (nearest the camera) and Lansdowne Parish Church of Scotland. St Mary's was erected in 1874, although the spire was not added until 1893. The architect was Sir George Gilbert Scott, and it was his son who completed the spire. Lansdowne Church was designed by John Honeyman in Early English Gothic style and built in 1862. Tramcar No. 520 was finally scrapped in 1959, having been in service since 1902.

Caledonian Mansions (right) were designed by James Miller and completed in 1895. Contrary to popular belief, the development was not an annexe to the Caledonian Railway's Central Hotel, but intended solely to generate rental income from the shops and flats above. Leishman & Son (right foreground) was a butcher's. The new high-level Great Western Bridge was opened in 1841, but by 1858 it had become apparent that the road was too narrow and not strong enough to carry the pipes for Glasgow's new water supply from Loch Katrine. To resolve this, the Loch Katrine water commissioners paid for widening and strengthening work to the bridge, which also made it possible for the road to accommodate Glasgow's tram network when it was introduced in 1872. The bridge was widened again in 1891, this time to designs by Bell & Miller, using steelwork from William Arrol's works at Dalmarnock.

Looking east along Great Western Road towards the entrance to the Botanic Gardens and Botanic Gardens Station in 1931. The station belonged to the Caledonian Railway and was opened in 1896. Designed by James Miller, it was built of bright red brick and had two tall towers topped by balconies with golden onion domes. The building was demolished in 1970 after a fire. At the left of the photograph is the steeple of what was Kelvinside (Botanic Gardens) Parish Church. The church secured its site at the price of eight shillings per square yard, opening in 1863 after occupying a temporary building at the corner of Byres Road and Observatory Road. The bells in the steeple were rung for the first time on Christmas Day 1917.

In the sixteenth century there were several mills on the River Kelvin. The 'Old Mill' was at the south-east end of the Old Bridge and is thought to have been built in 1136. When it burned down in 1836 the Bishop Mill, seen here on the right, was erected. It was powered by a water wheel until the 1950s when steam was introduced. Just left of centre is Scotstoun Mill, originally known as the Waulk Miln of Partick and built in 1507 for the preparation of woollen cloth. The Scotstoun family bought the mill in the late eighteenth century, but by 1834 it had been sold to John White and was being used as a flour and grain mill, with the current building on the site opened in 1877. To the left of Scotstoun Mill was the Regent Mill, so-named after the Regent Moray who gave it as a gift to the Incorporation of Bakers as a reward for supplying his army with bread during the 1568 campaign which ended with the Battle of Langside. It was destroyed by fire in 1886, but the shell was bought by John Ure and sold to the Scottish Co-operative Wholesale Society in 1903. After rebuilding it remained in operation until the 1970s when it was demolished. In 1800 the bridge seen here was widened, but in 1895 it was demolished and replaced by a new iron structure.

In 1903 Partick's Commissioners realised that vacant land in the burgh was being bought up at an alarming rate. Two sites were considered for a park in the east end of Partick: one in North Gardner Street and the other one, seen here, at Highburgh Road. Dowanhill School, in the background, was erected by Govan Parish School Board and opened in 1896. The site was bought from Dowanhill Estate Co. Ltd. and the school was built at a cost of £17,513. This included £630 for desks and furniture. Lord Balfour of Burleigh opened it and the first head teacher was Simon Fraser MA, whose annual stipend was £325 per annum. In order to increase the number of pupil places from 1,425 to 1,755, the architect was instructed to utilise the upper storey as classroom accommodation instead of art rooms, although the year the school opened average attendance was only 960. The tenements in the background are built of red sandstone, with older grey sandstone terraced houses at the left. At first tenements were built of grey sandstone, but by the early twentieth century nearby quarries were exhausted and red sandstone was being shipped in from Dumfriesshire or Arran.

Gardner Street was named after a butcher who was also a Partick Commissioner. In the 1920s, when motor shows came to Glasgow's Kelvin Hall, commercial vehicles used Gardner Street to demonstrate their hill-climbing capabilities. The church on the left was built as a replacement for an iron church called Partick Free Gaelic Church. With the union of the Free Church of Scotland and the United Presbyterian Church in 1900, permission was given for the congregation of the newly named Partick Gaelic United Free Church to build more substantial accommodation on the same site. The new church was finally opened in 1905, and the initial service saw the congregation stand to sing for the first time during public worship. The morning service was held in English and the 2 p.m. one in Gaelic. In the ten years between 1881 and 1891 the number of Gaelic speakers in Partick rose from 494 to 1,208.

The village of Anderston was named after an old Glasgow family, the Andersons of Stobcross and Dowhill. It was mainly occupied by weavers and became a burgh is 1824. Anderston Cross was the centre of the burgh, which only survived until 1846 before being swallowed up by Glasgow. This picture shows the impressive building which marked the Cross and stood at the junction with Argyle Street (right), along which

Opposite: The second half of the eighteenth century saw the spread of turnpike roads across Scotland – these were built by private developers who recouped their costs by charging tolls at various points. The system was successfully used to develop Scotland's road network, with particular emphasis on linking industrial centres such as Lanark, Blanytre, Greenock, Busby, Paisley,

a tram is travelling. An alternative mode of transport was offered by the low-level station, the entrance to which is at the left-hand side of the Cross building. Just behind the tenements above Anderston Cross was a music hall dating from the 1870s. Most of Anderston was demolished to make way for the Kingston Bridge and associated new roads, with only a very few of its old buildings remaining.

Thornliebank and Glasgow. The Round Toll stood at the junction of Garscube Road and Possil Road and probably dated from the late eighteenth or early nineteenth centuries. The building behind it was the Black Quarry School. Both landmarks disappeared in the 1870s when tolls were abolished, after which the corner site was redeveloped.

Most of the buildings in this 1938 photograph of St George's Cross were destroyed to make way for the M8 motorway. It was taken from the eastern end of Great Western Road looking into New City Road, with St George's Road leading to the left and right. The shops include Duncan's, Wood & Selby and Hoey's. The latter was founded in 1898 and had offices above the shop. To the left, just out of view, was Massey's the grocers, with Clarendon Halls behind it. Before Massey's took over the building there had been a bank on the site. The Empress Theatre, which became Jimmy Logan's Metropole in 1964, was located on St George's Road until its demolition in 1987.

Chapter 5
Charles Rennie Mackintosh and Kate Cranston

The reputation built up by Thomas Annan between 1855 and his death in 1887 meant that by the latter years of the nineteenth century his firm had become a household name. From the outset key clients included wealthy art collectors (generally rich businessmen), whom Annan visited in order to photograph their paintings and mansions. His portraits of Victorian luminaries further enhanced his status.

Like his father, James Craig Annan was a technically and artistically accomplished photographer who achieved significant recognition in his lifetime. While his brother John concentrated on the valuable commercial photography side of the business, James was a fine art photographer who was well-connected in Glasgow's creative circles. He exhibited his own photographs alongside those of contemporary artists, winning many awards, and also developed the firm's art dealing business.

In view of this pedigree it was perhaps inevitable that the Annans should come into contact with Charles Rennie Mackintosh and Kate Cranston, two of the most important figures in the development of contemporary architecture and interior design in Victorian Glasgow.

Key portraits of both figures were complemented by photographs of Mackintosh's School of Art and other architectural projects, including the interiors and exteriors of Kate Cranston's tea rooms. In the years since the photographs were taken many of these locations – particularly the interiors – have changed or been lost, making them of even greater value and interest to modern eyes.

Charles Rennie Mackintosh was born in 1868 in the Townhead district of Glasgow, and his family moved to Dennistoun when his policeman father was promoted. Mackintosh attended Allan Glen's school where he did not do well academically. Despite his father's disapproval, he trained as an architect and was apprenticed to John Hutchison in St Vincent Street, attending Glasgow School of Art in the evenings where he initially studied painting, then drawing. Mackintosh spent ten years at art school, during which time he won many prizes. He joined the firm of Honeyman & Keppie in 1889, and in 1892 his annual salary rose from £40 to £88, reflecting his value to the firm. In 1894 his salary increased again to £144. This photograph was taken at Gladsmuir, the home of William Davidson, who commissioned Windyhill at Kilmacolm from Charles Rennie Mackintosh. It shows Mackintosh with Davidson's son, Hamish, and was taken in 1898. At this time the first phase of building work at the Glasgow School of Art in Renfrew Street was underway, a project that Mackintosh described as 'a daily battle'.

Prior to 1906, Mackintosh lived in Mains Street, Blythswood (now Blythswood Street). His wife, Margaret Macdonald, had a private income of £250–£300 per year, and this financial independence allowed the couple to radically redesign the interior of their house. This picture shows the drawing room at Mains Street. Between 1906 and 1914 No. 6 Florentine Terrace (part of Ann Street and later renamed Southpark Avenue) became the Mackintoshs' home. They made substantial alterations to the interior of this house too, adding their own fireplaces, light fittings and wall- and floor-coverings. When war was declared the couple moved to London before finally settling in France in 1923. In 1920 they sold the house in Hillhead and its furniture to William Davidson, who lived there until his death in 1945. The University of Glasgow then acquired the property and used it as a professional residence for some time. As part of university expansion plans, the interiors were removed and reconstructed in the new Hunterian Art Gallery and the original house was then demolished.

In 1892 the governors of the Glasgow School of Art were seeking funding for a 'special building, fitted with modern requirements'. At that time the school was situated in the south-east corner of a block at Sauchiehall Street and Rose Street. By March 1896 sufficient funds had been raised for Francis Newbery (head of the school) to announce a competition for the design of a new building in Renfrew Street. The winners of that competition were the practice of Honeyman & Keppie, for whom Mackintosh worked. In May 1898 the foundation stone was laid, with the bill for the party afterwards coming to £66 (approximately £3,000 in today's terms).

The first phase of the school was opened on 20 December 1899, with the original costs being exceeded by more than a third. It took four years for the directors of the school to repay this overspend, by which time plans were being drawn up for the completion of the building. In 1907 Honeyman, Keppie & Mackintosh (as the firm was called by then) were appointed architects and work began, but perhaps not surprisingly under more careful financial scrutiny from the directors. The completed building opened in 1909 with Mackintosh this time clearly identified as its creator. The library (above) consists of three connected spaces: the library itself, its balcony and the store above. The latter has interior windows and the iron brackets from its ceiling support the floor and then connect with the posts beneath in the library. Its balcony features alternating panels that extend into the space below and are decorated with tiny ovals in columns. Thirteen specially designed lamps were installed in the centre of the library to enhance the building's natural light.

In 1896 Mackintosh embarked on the most enduring partnership of his professional career, joining forces with Kate Cranston in a business relationship that lasted until 1917. Catherine Cranston was born in 1849 and opened her first tea room in 1878, following in the footsteps of her brother Stuart, who started his career as a tea dealer. This evolved into a tea room when he began to offer bread and cakes as accompaniments to his tea tastings. The Cranston family were in the hotel business and Kate's father George owned the Crow Hotel in George Square. Her first venture was the Crown Tea Rooms, located in a temperance hotel in Argyle Street. By 1886 she had opened a second venture in Ingram Street. The Crown Tea Rooms were refurbished in 1888 by George Walton, brother of 'Glasgow Boy' artist Edward Walton. In 1894 Kate Cranston opened the Buchanan Street Tea Rooms (below and bottom) at Nos. 91–93 Buchanan Street, and although Walton designed the interiors the critically acclaimed wall murals were by Mackintosh.

Opposite: As her business empire expanded, Kate Cranston opened further new tea rooms in Sauchiehall Street, with Mackintosh in sole charge of the building, both externally and internally. The Willow Tea Rooms were opened on 29 October 1903 and achieved the critical acclaim that both Mackintosh and Cranston craved. The building featured a light ladies' tea room at the front, a darker general lunch room at the back, with a tea gallery above built around a well. The 'Salon de Luxe' on the first floor was a luxurious tea room that was considered a work of art in its own right.

With the Buchanan Street Tea Rooms running smoothly, Kate Cranston turned her attention to Argyle Street again, expanding and refurbishing her premises there. They reopened as shown above in 1899. When she extended her Ingram Street Tea Rooms the following year Mackintosh was solely responsible for the interior design of the premises. In 1901 Kate Cranston secured a concession at the International Exhibition.

In 1905 Kate Cranston commissioned Mackintosh to design a new tea room in the basement of her Argyle Street property. The result was the Dutch Kitchen, featuring a delft tiled fireplace with a rack for decorative plates, emerald green Windsor-style chairs, a black ceiling, mother-of-pearl squares on the columns and a black and white checked floor. Further commissions followed from his principal patron, but by 1913 Mackintosh had become a heavy drinker and was suffering from depression. He and

Margaret left Glasgow in 1914 and never returned, although Kate Cranston subsequently commissioned him to design an underground extension to the Willow Tea rooms. This was her last venture, and after her husband died in 1917 she sold her business and house (which had been remodelled by Mackintosh), moving into the North British Hotel in George Square. She left £64,476 on her death in 1934; by comparison, Mackintosh (who died of cancer of the tongue in 1928) left an estate valued at a mere £88.12s 6d.

The *Queen Empress* at Bridge Wharf, 1929.

Chapter 6
Shipbuilding and the Clyde

Until the latter part of the eighteenth century, the Clyde was only navigable as far as Glasgow by boats and lighters carrying cargoes of up to four or five tons. In 1768 the city magistrates called upon John Golborne of Chester to advise how the river could be improved and developed. He suggested dredging stones and hard gravel from the riverbed and narrowing the channel where it was too wide. Using these measures it was hoped that the Clyde could maintain a depth of four to five feet at the Broomielaw at low tide, allowing much larger vessels to use it. James Watt was also instructed to survey the river and found that it was as shallow as two feet at Dumbuck Ford, just above Dumbarton. Thus in 1770 an Act of Parliament was passed authorising the deepening of the channel to provide at least seven feet of water at every low tide. This goal had been achieved by 1775.

Further improvements to the river's navigability allowed larger and heavier vessels to reach the city, and by the beginning of the nineteenth century there were 382 yards of quayside at the Broomielaw, with approximately eight miles of quays within Glasgow Harbour.

Evidence of shipbuilding on the Clyde dates back to the 1300s, and in 1718 the first vessel for Atlantic use was launched near Port Glasgow. In 1818, following the deepening of the Clyde, John Barclay laid out the city's first shipyard at Stobcross Pool. Further yards were opened downstream at Whiteinch in the 1820s.

By the mid-1830s more than 36 steamships were offering passenger and goods services from Glasgow to destinations including Stranraer, Ayr, Campbeltown, Arrochar and Lochgilphead. As the railways expanded, the Glasgow, Paisley & Greenock Railway entered into an agreement with the Bute Steam Packet Company whereby their boats and trains would sail in connection with each other. In 1844 the railway company bought the steamboats *Isle of Bute* and *Maid of Bute*, going on to add three more steamers to their fleet. However, competition from private steamboat operators in Glasgow meant that this venture failed. The Caledonian Railway attempted a similar service in the early 1850s but this, too, failed.

In the 1820s Robert Napier and his cousin David became leaders in the design and construction of marine engines. David Napier owned a large engine- and boilerworks at Lancefield, near where the Scottish Exhibition and Conference Centre is now located. Beside the works was a basin where ships had their engines fitted. David Napier also took over an engineering works at Camlachie and went on to secure a contract for manufacturing water pipes for Glasgow Corporation. His marine engines were so good that two steamers fitted with them won a race in 1827 sponsored by the Northern Yacht Club. This brought him to the attention of Thomas Assheton Smith who, over a period of twenty years, ordered many steam yachts from him. David Napier's highly successful invention of the side-lever steeple engine in 1835 led him to move to London, where within two years his business had become 'very profitable', according to the Bank of Scotland. Robert Napier remained in Glasgow and he and his foreman, David Elder, trained future shipbuilders such as William Denny, John Elder and William Pearce. This picture shows the vessel *Persia* approaching completion at Robert Napier's yard in 1855.

Persia was built as the British and North American Royal Mail steamship and was launched on 3 July 1855 having cost £130,000. She was operated by the Cunard line, and was the first of the company's liners to be built from iron, rather than wood. When launched she was the largest vessel afloat, measuring 360 feet and weighing 3,400 tonnes. Her top speed exceeded thirteen knots and she had three masts, two funnels, two paddle wheels and a clipper bow. Within three months of her maiden voyage to New York in 1856, *Persia* had won the Blue Riband for the fastest crossing of the Atlantic in both directions. In 1857 she hit an iceberg but survived the collision relatively unscathed. This, of course, only served to enhance both Cunard's and Robert Napier's reputation. *Persia* continued to ply across the Atlantic until 1863 when her sister ship, *Scotia*, took over, after which she remained in service for four more years. She was sold in 1868 and after the removal of her engines was scrapped in 1872. A drawing of her interior and steam machinery was the only engineering drawing ever to be exhibited at the Royal Academy.

Initially rowing boats were used at intervals along the Clyde to transfer passengers between the north and south banks. As the river became busier, this became impractical and the Clyde Navigation Trustees began operating a vehicular ferry in 1857 which was purchased from Gilbert of Yorkhill. The route of the ferry was between Govan's Water Row and Pointhouse. Part of the purchase included an inn at Pointhouse which was demolished in 1909. The ferry could carry two carts, with horses, and moved across the river by means of a chain fixed between the banks which passed over a cog on the vessel. A steam ferry was introduced in 1867 and was able to carry three loaded carts, together with their horses and up to 80 passengers. It took the ferry 90 seconds to make the 450-foot crossing. By 1872 the ferries along the Clyde were carrying an average of 21,000 passengers every day and generating £10,000 of revenue annually. Another new ferry was introduced at Govan in 1875. This time it was a double-chain vessel, able to carry eight carts and 140 passengers, and is seen in this c.1900 picture at the slipway on the north bank of the river. The distinctive tower of Glasgow University is in the left background.

This picture of one of the graving (dry) docks at Govan dates from c.1928 and shows the *Cameronia* in the foreground with a City Line vessel to the left. There were three graving docks at Govan: the one nearest the river measured 551 feet; the middle one was 575 feet long; and the one furthest from the river was 880 feet in length. The docks, which were used for fitting out and repairing ships, were closed in 1988. Glasgow's first dry dock was built by Tod & McGregor at Meadowside in 1858, but the Clyde Navigation Trust was very keen to improve facilities on the river and Govan's first dry dock was opened in 1875, with the second following in 1886. Dry dock No. 3 cost £241,000 to build and opened in 1897. Despite being 880 feet long, 83 feet wide and nearly 27 feet deep, it could be drained in about two hours using four centrifugal pumps. *Cameronia* was built by William Beardmore & Co. in 1921 for the Anchor Line, and sailed the Glasgow–New York route at a service speed of sixteen knots. She was used as a troopship from 1940 to 1947, after which she was refitted as an Australian immigration ship. In 1953 she was renamed *Empire Clyde* and returned to use as a troopship. She was decommissioned in 1957 and broken up in Newport, south Wales.

Looking west along the Broomielaw in 1901, with Windmill Croft Quay visible on the south bank of the river. This had been operational since 1828, and for many years vessels belonging to Sloan & Co. departed to Belfast from here. The former quay is now part of a waterfront development by Laing Homes. The tower of the Sailors' Home can be seen at the far end of the Broomielaw.

Queen's Dock was built on land acquired by the Clyde Navigation Trust in the 1870s, and included the site of the Stobcross yard originally owned by Barclay Curle & Sons. 2,850,000 cubic yards of material had to be removed to create the dock, which covered an area of nearly 34 acres and incorporated 3,334 yards of quayside. Excluding the cost of the land, the dock cost £901,000 and was the largest in Scotland. The opening ceremony took place on 18 September 1877, and when it was announced that Queen Victoria had given permission for the dock to be named

after her 21 sticks of dynamite were exploded as a royal salute. The whole of the north quay was laid out as coal and mineral berths, with the central and southern quays given over to general cargo trade. The entrance to the dock featured a hydraulically operated horizontal swing bridge measuring 180 feet, designed to carry both rail and road traffic. In 1970 the dock closed to shipping, and in 1977 it was filled in using rubble from the demolition of St Enoch Station and a number of Victorian tenements. The Scottish Exhibition and Conference Centre was built on the site.

General Terminus Quay (seen here in 1957) opened in 1849 as a mineral berth, equipped with one hydraulic and two steam-powered cranes for lifting and tipping coal wagons. By 1855 these were handling 150,000 tons of coal per year, but after the Caledonian Railway took over the railway and loading facilities the quay's capacity was increased to 800,000 tons annually. By 1938 coal shipments had declined and the railway's successor suggested that the quay be developed for ore cargoes, but this plan was shelved when war broke out in 1939. In later years when Ravenscraig steelworks opened ore imports were expected to grow to 1.5 million tons, and in 1954 General Terminus Quay was the site chosen for the development needed to cope with this. Three giant cranes, built by Sir William Arrol, were erected on the site. Ten tons of ore could be handled at every grab, with a conveyor used to transport the ore to an adjacent road, and thence to a 14,000-ton storage bunker. As ore carriers got bigger and bigger the terminal moved to a deep-water berth at Hunterston and in 1979 the three cranes at General Terminus Quay were dismantled.

Although John Brown's yard (seen here in 1956) was latterly in Clydebank, it had its origins in Finnieston. In 1847 James and George Thomson began a marine engineering business after working for Robert Napier. They established their venture in Clyde Bank Foundry and in 1851 expanded by setting up a shipyard at Bankton, east of Govan. By 1871 the firm was under the management of James Rodger Thomson, George's son. He purchased land at Barns of Clyde, diagonally opposite the confluence with the Cart, and the shipyard was transferred from Govan, bringing with it the name Clyde Bank, later to be taken by the town that grew up around it. In 1899 the business was taken over by John Brown & Co. of Sheffield, who were chosen by Cunard to build passenger liners including *Lusitania* and *Aquitania*. A contract was signed for a new liner, No. 534, the *Queen Mary*, in 1930. She was followed by a larger sister ship, *Queen Elizabeth*. The last famous ship was launched in 1967 – the Cunard liner *Queen Elizabeth II* – although John Brown's stayed in business until 2001 by building oil rigs and modules for oil exploration.

Dalmuir Dock showing (left to right) HMS *Fairy*, HMS *Argonaut*, HMS *Hermes*, RMS *Carrsbrook Castle*, SS *Regele Carol I* and SY *Atmah*. After taking over David Napier's yard at Govan in 1900, William Beardmore purchased land at Dalmuir, opening a yard there in 1906 with the launch of the battleship *Agamemnon*. Despite difficulties in securing contracts because older companies had long-standing contracts with shipping lines, Beardmore's managed to secure Admiralty work. In addition to ships, the company also built submarines, aircraft, airships and tanks, as well as making mines, guns, and fuses for shells. By the end of the First World War Beardmore's employed 13,000 workers at Dalmuir. After the war part of the Dalmuir works was given over to locomotive repair and construction. The business suffered when the Washington Naval Treaty was signed in 1922 and the world's major powers agreed that no new warships – the very type of ship that Beardmore's was best suited to – would be built for the next ten years. The yard closed in 1931.

Chapter 7

The Clyde coast

Before the development of the railways – and in an era when roads were poor – waterborne transport was one of the principal means of getting to coastal locations in the west of Scotland. Perhaps born out of this early transport necessity, Glaswegians have always had a great fondness for trips 'doon the watter'. In the steamship era most small boys could identify vessels by their colours, flags and funnel arrangements, and a fortnight's holiday to a resort on the Clyde coast was once considered the ultimate summer holiday.

By the 1870s the bulk of the city's river traffic was departing from the Broomielaw. The North British Steam Packet Co. operated a service to Dunoon and Holy Loch Piers, while Williamson's fleet sailed to Rothesay and Port Bannatyne from Prince's Pier. At Wemyss Bay Gillies & Campbell offered services to Port Bannatyne, Rothesay and Millport, while Arran traffic was taken by the Glasgow & South Western Railway to Ardrossan and thence by privately owned steamers to Lamlash and Brodick. Troon, Ayr, Largs, Saltcoats,

Garelochhead and Campbeltown were other popular destinations.

The steamers enjoyed their heyday between 1889 and 1914 when Glaswegians streamed out of the city in droves, particularly during the Glasgow Fair when trips to the Clyde coast were especially popular. Rivalry between the captains of paddle steamers was common, with strong pressure to arrive first at a particular destination (which also meant departing promptly for the return trip!). In 1890 the *Duchess of Hamilton* left Brodick Pier while passengers were still embarking, steaming off with the gangway still in place and passengers hanging over the edge. Collisions were not uncommon.

The increasing affordability of foreign travel, combined with greater car ownership, meant that an extensive steamer network eventually ceased to be viable. Although the Clyde Coast towns have never regained the enormous popularity of their heyday, they are still well-served by public transport, with train services from Glasgow connecting with ferries to the islands.

The steamers *Mercury* and *Benmore* at Rothesay. *Mercury* was launched on 18 April 1892 for the Glasgow & South Western Railway, achieving a speed of 18.45 knots in her trials over the Skelmorlie measured mile. This made her even faster than her sister ship *Neptune*. At Rothesay on 20 July 1893, just as *Mercury* was about to leave the pier, a man with a two-year-old child fell into the water. The *Glasgow Herald* reported that a young man named Joseph Maguire immediately jumped from the pier to the paddlebox and grabbed the man, who had been stunned by a blow to the head. After helping to pull him out, Maguire dived into the water and rescued the child. A large subscription was collected from the passengers and presented to the rescuer by the captain. *Mercury* was broken up in 1933. In 1884 *Benmore* was bought from Captain Robert Campbell by Captain William Buchanan as part of the Buchanan fleet. She was a classic Victorian steamer with a raised quarterdeck, single engine and low-pressure haystack boiler. In 1923 she was broken up.

Rothesay has been described as both 'the Montpellier of Scotland' and 'Glasgow by the Sea', presumably depending on the point of view of the writer! It is the ancestral home of the Stuart kings in Scotland and lies on the Highland Boundary Fault. Bute is fifteen miles long and about four miles wide, and has been inhabited for at least 5,500 years. The first steamboat service to the island commenced in 1814, making Rothesay three and a half hours journey from Glasgow. At the peak of the tourist trade, up to 100 steamers a day berthed at the pier, bringing thousands of holidaymakers to Bute. A family could rent a living room and kitchen for as little as £6 a fortnight, though often they had to spend the first night outdoors because of the pressures on accommodation. The land on which the front of the town is built was reclaimed from the sea in the mid-nineteenth century, before which the shoreline was 200 metres further inland, not far from the castle. This picture shows Victoria Street.

Fair Saturday was the busiest day of the year for trips 'doon the watter', with Largs, seen here in 1900, the destination for many holidaymakers. The town is famous for the Battle of Largs of 1263, which took place when King Haakon's fleet was blown ashore by a fierce gale and resulted in him being forced to retreat after two days of fighting. A Viking-related festival is still held every year.

After the Battle of Largs, the island of Cumbrae became part of Scotland again, having been captured by the Vikings when they invaded. From 1800 a fast customs cutter was based at Millport, the main settlement on Cumbrae, since it was a good location from which to monitor shipping passing through the Clyde estuary. Millport boasts the smallest cathedral in Europe, with seating for only 100 worshippers. After studying at Oxford the 6th Lord Glasgow

Largs takes its name from *Learg*, meaning hillside, and is the port for Cumbrae, a mile across the water. Lord Kelvin lived in the town at Netherhall from 1874 until his death in 1907. The railway reached Largs in 1885, providing an alternative to the steamer services from Glasgow. Today most people know Largs for Nardini's art deco cafe and restaurant, famous for its ice cream.

was determined to invigorate the Episcopalian Church in Scotland, and in particular on Cumbrae, since it was owned by his family. In 1849 he funded the establishment of a theological college in Millport, and this was opened in 1851, with the Cathedral of the Isles consecrated in 1876. Its 123-foot spire is over three times the length of the nave and six times its width. This picture shows the harbour at Millport.

Until the 1700s the separate villages of Kames and Kirkton overlooked different ends of the bay, but over the years they gradually grew together and became known as Millport, which grew up beside the harbour, as seen here.

The captain of the island's customs cutter built a mansion on the seafront called the Garrison, since barracks had stood on the site in 1745. It was extended in 1819 when it became the family home of Lord Glasgow.

In 1812 the world's first ocean-going steamer, the *Comet*, was also the first steam-powered vessel to visit Millport. Lord Glasgow built a pier at Millport in 1833 and it was this that paved the way for a steady influx of visitors to the island for years to come. In the 1920s the town boasted 26 sweet shops, while more recently Travis wrote *Why Does It Always Rain On Me* when staying there.

Enjoying the warming effects of the Gulf Stream and situated within easy reach of Glasgow, Troon became a popular seaside destination, as testified by the bathing machines and donkeys seen here! The Ayrshire coast is one of the sunniest parts of the western mainland of Scotland and the 1,381 hours of sunshine recorded annually for Troon between 1931 and 1960 was equivalent to that enjoyed by central London. The town also has the lowest rainfall of the west coast of Britain. Troon was home to the Ailsa Shipbuilding Co. from 1887 to 1986, but is probably best known for its golf course, Royal Troon. Arthur Havers, then professional at Coombe Hill, won the first Open at Troon in 1923, but it was Arnold Palmer's second successive win there in 1962 that helped restore interest in the championship amongst American professionals. The 133rd Open Championship was held in Troon in 2004.